WAX AND CASTING

A Notebook of Jewelry Design and Technique

Roger Armstrong

Savannah College of Art
Savannah, Georgia

Edinboro University of Pennsylvania
Edinboro, Pennsylvania

PUBLISHING COMPANY

Star
PUBLISHING COMPANY
P.O. Box 68
Belmont, CA 94002

> TO:
>
> Those I learned from
> and
> those I helped to learn
> and
> sons Tom and Scott
> and N. and R.
> who are teaching me
> things I never knew.

Cover Design: Roger Armstrong
Illustrations: Jonathon Herbruck
              Scott Easton
              Roger Armstrong
Production Coordinator: Cheryl Baca
Typesetter: Beverly Page

Roger Armstrong
Savannah College of Art, / Edinboro University,
Savannah, Georgia / Edinboro, Pennsylvania

M.A.	University of New Mexico
M.F.A.	Cranbrook Academy of Art
M.S.	Florida State University
Member	The Society of North American Goldsmiths

Printed in the United States of America
ISBN: 0-89863-038-X

CONTENTS

Preface v

CHAPTER 1: DESIGN ATTITUDES 1

CHAPTER 2: METALS 9

CHAPTER 3: THE WAX 17

CHAPTER 4: TOOLS 27

               Hand Tools 27

               Tools for Waxing 37

CHAPTER 5: TORCHES FOR CASTING 47

CHAPTER 6: WAX TECHNIQUES 53

               Wax Sheet Fabrication 55

               Finishing the Wax 74

CHAPTER 7: STONE SETTING 75

               Mounts 80

               Prongs 88

               Casting Gems in Place 90

CHAPTER 8: GEM STONE CASTABILITY 93

CHAPTER 9: SPRUEING 97

               Sprueing the Model 97

               Weigh the Model 103

CHAPTER 10: INVESTING 105

               Mounting 105

               Debubblizing 106

               The Process of Investing 109

CHAPTER 11:   BURNOUT 119

CHAPTER 12:   THE CASTING PROCESS 133

                    Casting Preparation Broken Arm Machine 133

                    Casting Preparation Straight Arm Machine 139

                    Casting 141

                    Pouring the Metal 145

                    Safety 147

CHAPTER 13:   INVESTMENT AND SPRUE REMOVAL 149

CHAPTER 14:   THE FINISHING OF CAST JEWELRY 153

                    Finishing the Casting 157

CHAPTER 15:   GRAVITY CASTING 165

                    Burnout 173

                    Preparation of the Flask 174

                    Finishing the Gravity Casting 175

              Appendices 179

              Index 189

PREFACE

This notebook is developed from lectures and demonstrations spanning twenty-five years of teaching. Full of tips and sage advice, the wide variety of wax and casting techniques that are covered have been developed or discovered by students, fellow jewelers, and myself through practice and application.

The techniques in this notebook are sequentially organized for your skills to grow and stack one upon the other. The simple structure of the text is designed to make the processes and procedures both easy-to-find and comfortable to follow. Procedures are generally kept to the open or facing pages. No flipping pages in the middle of a process, and the spiral binding allows the book to lay flat when open!

This is a book that records ways of doing things. The background grid on each page will give you a structure to change or add information that you experience or discover. It is important that you record your experiences, for only then can you repeat them with consistency. These records of changes not only give you a report of your growth, but they help you to repeat or avoid specific actions.

The opening chapter discusses a type of design philosophy and the importance of a personal vision, which I believe is very individual and private to each artist. In subsequent chapters, only processes and techniques are presented. What you do with the techniques will be of your design visions, not mine. The goal: To develop confidence in your craftsmanship as an artist!

May your castings never pit.
May your saw blades never dull.
May you and your art grow with strength and grace.

Roger Armstrong

DESIGN ATTITUDES

Design is the result of an idea.

Design is the result of organization.

It is the physical organization that results in

visual organization of art elements.

Or sometimes,

it is the visual organization that results in

physical organization of Art Elements!!

Design is a personal opinion.

When you get enough people together that have the same opinion you have an emergence of a style or school of art.

The "FORM FOLLOWS FUNCTION" of European roots is expressed in our culture as

separated, mechanical, or

having a hard visual edge.

EXAMPLES:

A ring band fits the finger and provides a stand for the decoration.

The function of a spoon is to hold something in its bowl.

The function of a buckle is to secure.

The function of a symbol is to inform.

A reaction to this attitude was

form without function or

function from an unlikely form.

EXAMPLES:

A spoon with a hole in the bowl.

A buckle with spikes pointed at the wearer.

A nonsense symbol in a form that should have meaning.

A development of these two attitudes was

the environmental attitude where

function and decoration and environment blended together.

EXAMPLES:

A spoon not only held something in the bowl, but was comfortable to hold.

It was also a decorative form that blended into and became part of the environment of the table.

The reaction to this attitude was:

The development of forms that are made to be in direct contrast to its environment.

EXAMPLES:

The environment becomes the display stand to show the piece.

The piece stands out and commands attention.

DESIGN POSSIBILITIES

earrings	epaulet	reliquary	fondue forks
pins	nose plug	challis	salad service
studs	buttons	small sculpture	lockets
chains	cuff links	knobs	hair pins
combs	collar clips	pendants	buckles
necklaces	money clips	pocket knives	bracelets
belts	door knobs	chest handles	hat bands
rings	door hinges	kitchen tools	gavels
metals	chest hinges	wood working tools	table service
pill boxes	tiaras	toys	table ware
lunch boxes	charms	coin banks	wall pieces
eye glasses	beads	cigarette cases	

The list is endless. In many of these categories you can add many individual items. There is history to draw from for ideas as well as your future.

When you design consider when the piece will be worn and the use.

Consider the purpose of the piece.

EXAMPLES:

formal wear	show piece	wear special occasions
casual	small sculpture	wear strenuous activity
nonwearable	wear every day	universal wear

When you design consider the function.

The function of a buckle is to secure and

adorn,

give status and

inform.

The function of a spoon:

is to hold,

to be held,

to give status,

to inform and/or

decorate.

The function of a ring is to:

fit,

show status,

inform and/or

accent.

The function of a nonfunctional object:

is not to function in its normal context.

It is to define,

inform,

exist and

surprise.

The function of a symbol is to:

    evoke response

    inform and

    control.

The function of a toy is to:

    entertain,

    amuse,

    decorate,

    instruct and

    challenge.

Consistency is a key concept!

Design lines within and about your piece to

    demonstrate the consistency of your idea.

        The rounds should be round
        if that is what you intend them to be.

        The flats are flat
        with no question to the fact allowed.

        Make it look deliberate.

        Make it look crisp and sharp.

        Make it be positive.

Give your idea rhythmic repetition through the association of forms and

give it interest through variety of

    plane,

    shape,

    line,

    texture,

    balance,

    color,

    reflective quality,

    light and dark.

All of the factors are controlled by your

  decision making ability and

  problem solving ability.

    Is it clean?

    Slick?

    Organic?

    Bumpy?

    Dangerous?

    Sharp?

    Functionally sound?

There are two basic design approaches.

In the *intuitive mode:*

> You define your concept as a vision/mental image.
>
> You build toward that vision,
>
> > changing the object to fit the vision or
> >
> > changing the vision to fit the object.
>
> Wax lends itself to this approach;
>
> > you can start with a concept and
> >
> > let it grow to be itself.

In the *structured mode:*

> You define your concept as a vision/mental image.
>
> You freeze the concept on paper as a sketch or drawing.
>
> You control the growing
>
> > by working from a pattern or the drawing.

Both approaches are valid.

There was an art education study done in the early '60s. An interview of 50 artists per each media was conducted involving drawing, painting, jewelry, ceramics, sculpture, print, enameling and design. Most of the areas were equally divided between working intuitively or structured. Some artists said they do both. Some artists said they would like to do both.

If your approach works in aiding you to achieve your goals, it is valid. If you struggle and fight your vision, maybe you should approach your vision from a different direction.

Craftsmanship is an attitude.

It is an awareness of all the minute factors.

It is a consistent attitude suited to the piece.

It is a total visual effect.

It is an appropriate and consistent aesthetic.

It is a statement of control.

It is a statement of purpose.

One hundred percent of the original vision/mental image is seldom obtained.

In the making there are too many decisions to be made that develop into changes from the vision.

Stay flexible

You have the option to change the vision to match the decision change.

This way you can obtain 80% of the vision.

But ...

it is that 100% goal

that keeps us making jewelry

that keeps us making our art.

2

METALS

There are two weight systems for metals:

troy weight for gold, silver, platinum

avoirdupois weight for copper, brass, bronze, aluminum, nickel, silver and lead.

Troy

24 gr (grains) equals 1 dwt (penny weight)

20 dwt equals 1 oz (ounce)

12 oz equals 1 lb (pound)

Avoirdupois

$27\frac{1}{3}$ gr equals 1 gram

16 grams equals 1 oz

16 oz equals 1 lb

The troy ounce is about 10% heavier.

Troy ounces $\times$ 1.0971 = avoirdupois ounces.

Avoirdupois $\times$ 0.9115 = troy ounces.

1 oz avoirdupois = 28.25 grams.

1 oz troy = 31.125 grams.

It's important to know the properties of the various metals you work with.

To test for silver:

File a deep notch in the piece to be tested.

Apply a drop of nitric acid to the notch.

Coin silver will turn darkish or black.

Nickel silver will turn green.

Sterling silver will turn cloudy cream.

Fine silver, when heated to light red heat and cooled, stays white.

Sterling, under the same conditions, turns black.

Fine silver—melting temperature 1762° F.

Is sometimes called 'three nine.'

Should be 99.9% pure.

Is very ductile.

Work hardens.

Anneals at 900° F.

Air cool to warm then quench.

Malleable.

Used as a surface for enamels and for bezels.

Can be ordered in sheet or wire.

For best color match use IT or hard solder.

Sterling silver–melting temperature 1640° F.

   92½% fine silver and 7½% pure copper.

   White in color.

   Ductile.

   Tarnished by sulphur.

   Malleable.

   Work hardens.

   Anneals at 1200° F.

   Air cool until black then quench.

   Most common metal used in craft jewelry.

   Can be ordered in sheet, wire, and hardness.

   Can be ordered annealed (standard if not specified).

   Hard and half-hard used for findings.

   Spring-hard used for money clips, tie bars, etc.

Coin silver–melting temperature 1615° F.

   90% fine silver and 10% pure copper.

   White in color.

   Ductile, but harder than sterling.

   Malleable, but stiffer than sterling.

   Tarnished by sulphur.

   Work hardens rapidly.

   Anneals at 1200° F.

   Air cool until black then quench.

Nickel silver–melting temperature 2030° F.

   Known as German silver.

   18% nickel, no silver.

   65% copper, 17% zinc.

   Gray white in color.

   Ductile but harder than sterling.

   Malleable.

   Work hardens rapidly.

   Anneals at 1200° F.

   Air cool until black then quench.

   Tarnished by sulphur.

   Solders with all silver solders.

24 karat (kt) fine gold–melting temperature 1945° F.

   Most malleable and ductile of all metals.

   Can be hammered into paper-thin sheets.

   Anneals at 1200° F.

   Air cool to hot then quench.

   Work hardens slowly.

   Does not tarnish.

   Used as an anode in plating.

The other karat or karat golds are numbered by the parts of 24 kt gold they contain:

   22 kt gold is 22 parts 24 kt gold, 2 parts other metals.

   20 kt gold is 20 parts 24 kt gold, 4 parts other metals.

   18 kt gold is 18 parts 24 kt gold, 6 parts other metals.

14 kt gold is 14 parts 24 kt gold, 10 parts other metals.

10 kt gold is 10 parts 24 kt gold, 14 parts other metals.

Generally, the higher the karat the softer and more malleable the metal.

10 kt used for objects subject to heavy wear such as men's rings and belt buckles.

14 kt used for most of the gold alloys.

18 kt used for women's jewelry.

22 kt used for women's jewelry, European and Asian attitude.

24 kt gold is naturally a bright yellow used in minimum wear situations.

Yellow gold is most widely used.

White gold would be next in popularity.

It is very hard, very brittle.

Will not cause copper reaction.

18 kt hard white melts at 1730° F.

18 kt medium white melts at 1697° F.

18 kt soft white melts at 1669° F.

14 kt hard white melts at 1767° F.

14 kt medium white melts at 1690° F.

14 kt soft white melts at 1625° F.

10 kt hard white melts at 1580° F.

These are various colors of 18 kt gold and are 75% 24 kt by weight.

Red gold: copper 25%.

Rose gold: copper 22¼%, fine silver 2¾%.

Light gold: copper 20%, fine silver 5%.

Pale (pearl) gold: fine silver 15%, copper 10%.

Signet bright English gold: fine silver 12¼%, copper 12¼%.

Deep rich yellow gold: copper 15¼%, fine silver 9½%.

Green gold: fine silver 25%.

Platinum—melting point 3223° F.

Grayish white in color.

Very ductile.

Very malleable.

Does not tarnish.

Used primarily for diamond sets because of its color, strength and malleability.

Copper—melting point 1980° F.

Annealed at dull red.

Very malleable.

Tarnishes easily.

Work hardens.

Used as a primary metal for enameling.

Working properties similar to silver.

Anneals at 1200° F.

Air cool until black then quench.

Can be cast if design is blocky without many holes.

Commercial copper is alloy of 99.8% copper, 0.2% arsenic.

Bronze–melting point 1634° F.

    An alloy of copper and tin.

    Alloy used for coins or sculpture: 95% copper, 5% tin.

    Work hardens.

    Anneals at 1250° F.

    Air cool until black then quench.

    Casts very well.

    Forges well.

Brass–melting point 1780° F.

    An alloy of copper and zinc.

    Difficult to forge.

    Not ductile.

    Tends to crack.

    Anneals at 1200° F.

    Keep at temperature for 5 minutes to anneal fully.

    Can quench immediately.

    Work hardens easily and quickly.

    Anneal often.

    Casts well.

3

THE WAX

Wax Sheets:

    A group of waxes with similar characteristics.

    Has a melting range 150° F to 162° F.

    Is transparent enough to trace patterns.

    Cut in shapes for pendants, pins, earrings, etc.

    Cut in strips for ring bands.

    Use heat and blue or green wax

       to attach and join shapes.

    Warm the wax to form it.

       Use a lamp with 40 watt bulb 4″ to 12″ away.

       The best temperature range is 85° F to 100° F.

    Warm the wax to take impressions.

    It is smoothable when brushed with a flame.

    Bonds together easily.

    Cut with a very warm tool.

    Cut while wax is warm.

Pink Base Plate Wax:

 3″ × 6″ in 14 gauge.

 Melts at 155° F (approximately).

 Flexible when warm, 85° F.

 Easily molded.

 Brittle when cool, 65° F.

 Good for ring bands.

Pink Casting Wax Sheets:

 3″ × 5½″ in 22, 24, 26, 28, 30 and 32 gauge.

 Melts 156° F (approximately).

 Flexible when warm 90° F.

 Brittle when cool 65° F.

Pink Set Up Wax:

 5⅝″ × 2⅞″ in 16 gauge.

 Two grades:

  Regular is winter grade.

   Medium soft.

   Flexible at room temperature, 72° F.

  Hard is summer grade.

   Medium hard at room temperature, 72° F.

   Flexible, pliable when heated to 95° F.

  Both grades brittle when cool, 60° F.

Pink Sheet Wax:

5" × 3" in ½ mm (23 ga), 1 mm (18 ga), 1½ mm (15 ga), 2 mm (12 ga) and 3 mm (8 ga).

Flexible at room temperature, 70° F.

Very flexible and formable when warmed, 95° F.

Brittle when cool, 60° F.

Pink Sheet Wax:

5⅞" × 2⅞" in 1 mm (18 ga), 2 mm (12 ga) and 3 mm (8 ga).

Flexible at room temperature, 70° F.

Brittle when cool, 60° F.

Pink Sheet Wax:

4" × 4" in 14, 16, 18, 20, 22, 24, 26 and 28 gauge.

Flexible at room temperature 70° F.

Very flexible and formable when warm 95° F.

Brittle when cool 60° F.

Blue Preformed Wax Shapes:

Comes in many shapes and gauges.

Melts at 167° F.

Flexible at room temperature, 75° F.

Once melted, becomes hard and brittle.

Always softens under heat.

Put under light, 85° F.

Primary wax for construction.

Blue is used to give strength:

as brace,

as texture,

to pink and green wax.

Square, 4″ long sticks come in

6, 8, 10, 12 and 14 gauge.

Triangular, 4″ long sticks come in

8, 10, 12 and 14 gauge.

Bezel, 4″ long sticks come in

6, 8 and 10 gauge.

Uncut bezel, 4″ long sticks come in

2, 4, 6, 8 and 10 gauge.

Half-round, 4″ long sticks and ¼ lb or ½ lb spool come in

6, 8, 10, 12 and 14 gauge.

Round, 4″ long sticks and ¼ lb or ½ lb spool come in

6, 8, 10, 12, 14, 16, 18, 20 and 22 gauge.

Green Casting Wax Sheets:

5½″ × 3″ in 22, 24, 26, 28 and 30 gauge.

Melts at 160° F.

Very flexible at room temperature, 70° F.

Very soft (almost sticky) when warmed, 90° F.

Flexible when cool, 60° F.

Brittle when cold, 40° F.

Green Sticky Wax Sheets:

    6″ × 3″ in 18 gauge.

    Very soft, plastic, sticky at room temperature, 70° F.

    Used to fill in hollows without heat.

    Used to attach models to sprue formers.

    Used to attach two waxes together.

    Little change in flexibility after heating.

Green Preformed Wax Shapes:

    Comes in several shapes and gauges.

    Very flexible at room temperature, 70° F.

    Melts at 160° F.

    Once melted becomes hard and brittle.

    Always softens with heat, 85° F.

    4″ long sticks.

    Half-round

        6, 8, 10, 12 and 14 gauge.

    Round

        6, 8, 10, 12, 14, 16, 18 and 20 gauge.

    Pear

        6 gauge.

    Square

        10 gauge.

    Triangular

        12 gauge.

Master Pattern Wax:

Used for carving.

Used for tooling.

Used for machining.

High melting point, 203° F to 229° F.

Difficult to build up.

Difficult to use for trailing.

Hard wax is formulated to

shave cleanly and

resist sticking to cutting tool.

Comes in 1 lb blocks.

Comes in sliced 1 lb blocks.

Comes shaped in solid ring rods,

6 inches long,

outside diameter $\frac{7}{8}$" and $1\frac{1}{16}$".

Comes shaped in round center hole tube

6 inches long,

center hole $\frac{5}{8}$" diameter,

outside diameter $\frac{7}{8}$" and $1\frac{1}{16}$".

Comes as shaped round tube with off center hole

6 inches long,

hole $\frac{5}{8}$" diameter,

outside diameter $1\frac{1}{16}$".

Comes as shaped flat top tube

    6 inches long,

    hole ⅝″ diameter.

Comes in different sizes:

    1″ h × 1″ w,

    1⅛″ h × 1″ w,

    1⅜″ h × 1⅛″ w and

    1⅜″ h × 1¼″ w.

Red Master Pattern Wax:

  Melts at 203° F.

  Medium soft.

  Easy carving.

  Can use for machining.

Blue Master Pattern Wax:

  Melts at 220° F.

  Medium hard.

  Good to carve.

  Good for machining.

Green Master Pattern Wax:

  Melts at 229° F.

  Hard wax.

  Best to use for machining.

  Difficult to hand carve.

File and Carving Wax:

Best for hand carving.

Blue Wax:

Medium hard.

Melts at 203° F.

Purple Wax:

Medium hard.

Melts at 165° F.

Green Wax:

Hard.

Melts at 200° F.

Blue Filing Wax:

Soft.

Melts at 155° F.

Buildup or Trailing Wax:

Used to build up layers of wax.

All have good flexibility,

good carvability,

good workability,

and are excellent for trailing or lay up

using hot trailing tools

or cool carving tools.

Perfect Purple Wax:

    Comes in 2 oz blocks.

    Melts at 165° F.

    Has a moderate flow.

Wax Pen Wax:

    Comes in ¼ lb box,

        as 4″ × 8 ga sticks.

    Melts at 162° F

        with moderate flow.

Red Injection Wax:

    Comes in 1 lb stick

    or ¼ lb block.

    Can also buy as chips by the pound.

    Melts at 160° F.

    Has a slow flow.

Green Pattern Wax:

    Melts at 229° F.

    Has a very slow flow.

Blue Wax Wire Sticks and

Blue Wax in Bulk:

    Comes in 6 gauge.

    Melts at 167° F.

    Has a fast flow.

TOOLS

HAND TOOLS

Of course you need all the usual hand tools that are needed to make jewelry.

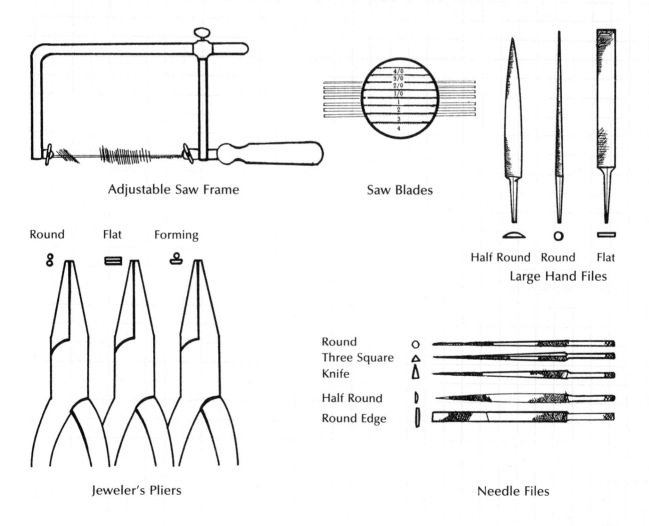

Adjustable Saw Frame

Saw Blades

Half Round   Round   Flat
Large Hand Files

Round   Flat   Forming

Jeweler's Pliers

Round
Three Square
Knife
Half Round
Round Edge

Needle Files

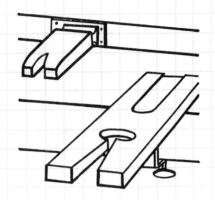

Bench Pin or 'V' Board and Clamp

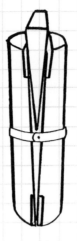

Ring Clamp

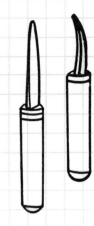

Burnisher

Drill bits come in the following sizes:
  #30—exactly 8 gauge
  #37—exactly 10 gauge
  #45—larger than 12 gauge
  #46—exactly 12 gauge
  #50—larger than 14 gauge
  #51—exactly 14 gauge
  #54—larger than 16 gauge
  #55—exactly 16 gauge
  #58—larger than 18 gauge
  #59—exactly 18 gauge
  #66—larger than 20 gauge
  #67—exactly 20 gauge
  #71—exactly 22 gauge
  #75—exactly 24 gauge
  #78—exactly 26 gauge
  #80—exactly 28 gauge

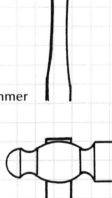

Chasing Hammer

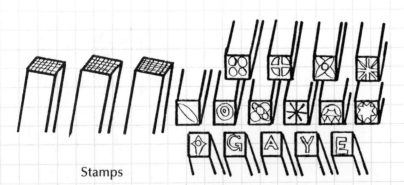

Stamps

Ball Pein Hammer

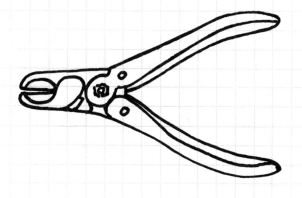

Sprue Cutter With Compound Action

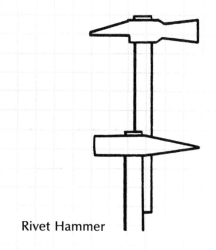

Rivet Hammer

Heavy Sprue Cutter (Bolt Cutter)

Ring Mandrels

Make your own ring mandrels from

    wood,

    plastic or

    aluminum.

Cast them in brass or bronze.

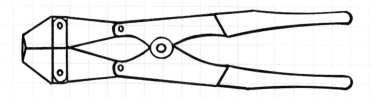

Ring Mandrels

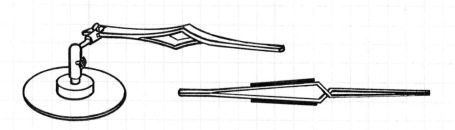

Third Hand and Crosslock Tweezer

Stone Setting Burrs

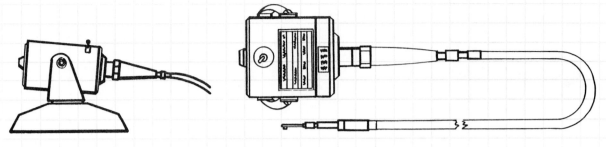

Flexible Shafts, E and D Series

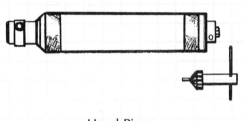

Hand Piece

The EE series of flexible shaft has a reduction gear to "step down" the speed of the shaft from 16,000 rpm to 5,000 rpm. Some attachments require that speed limitation.

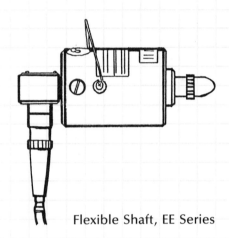

Flexible Shaft, EE Series

Tools for Flexible Shaft

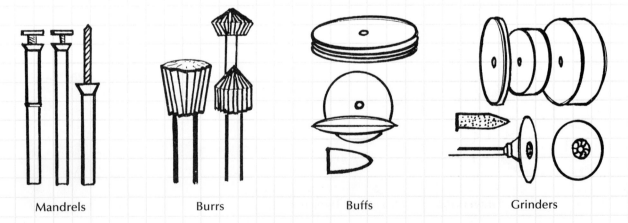

Mandrels   Burrs   Buffs   Grinders

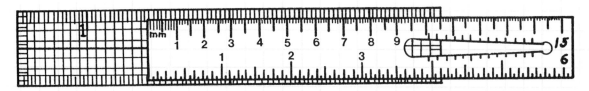

Straight Edge

Balance Scale

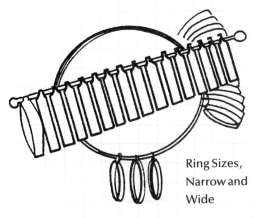

Ring Sizes,
Narrow and
Wide

Brown & Sharpe Gauge

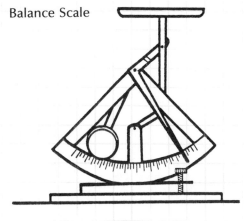

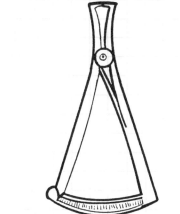

Douziemen Gauge (Measures in Tenths of mm.)

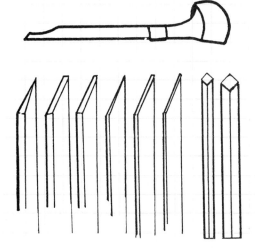

Engravers

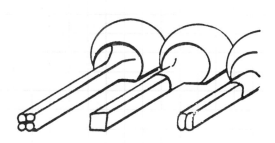

Stone Pusher

This vibrating table uses a ¼ hp motor with ¾ of its pully cut away. You can use a smaller motor if you wish.

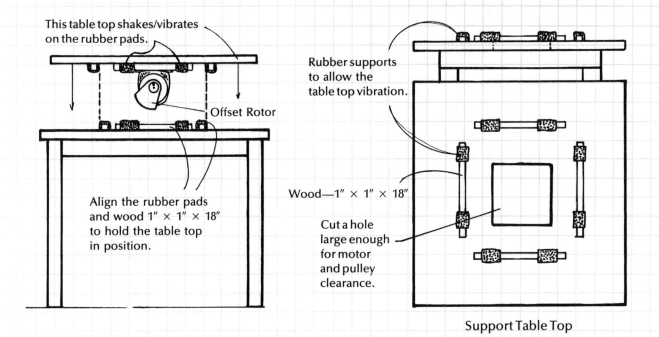

This table top shakes/vibrates on the rubber pads.

Offset Rotor

Align the rubber pads and wood 1″ × 1″ × 18″ to hold the table top in position.

Rubber supports to allow the table top vibration.

Wood—1″ × 1″ × 18″

Cut a hole large enough for motor and pulley clearance.

Support Table Top

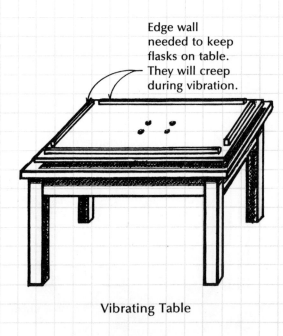

Edge wall needed to keep flasks on table. They will creep during vibration.

Vibrating Table

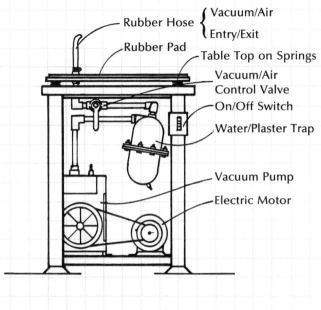

Rubber Hose
{ Vacuum/Air
Entry/Exit
Rubber Pad
Table Top on Springs
Vacuum/Air Control Valve
On/Off Switch
Water/Plaster Trap
Vacuum Pump
Electric Motor

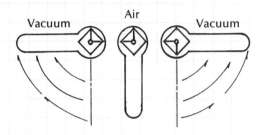

Vacuum
Air
Vacuum

Vacuum/Air Control Valve Positions

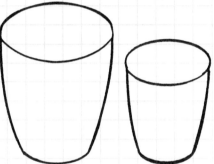

Rubber Mixing Bowls

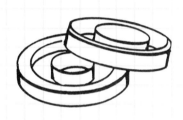

Rubber Sprue Bases

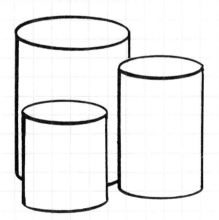

Stainless Steel Flasks

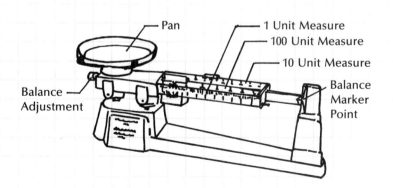

Pan
1 Unit Measure
100 Unit Measure
10 Unit Measure
Balance Marker Point
Balance Adjustment

Triple Beam Balance Scale

Vacuum Casters

There are several kinds on the market.

They basically are the same variation aiding gravity casting.

The flask is placed on a platform over a vacuum port. Metal is introduced to the flask as vacuum is applied to the bottom of the flask. The air pressure (14 lbs per square inch) forces the metal into the mold.

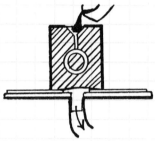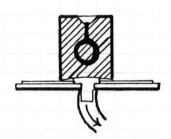

Some models of the vacuum casting machines use an air pressure cap that applies vacuum at the bottom of the flask at the same time air pressure is applied to the top. In this system the melt is made directly in the button funnel.

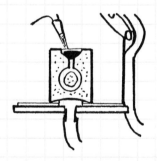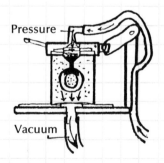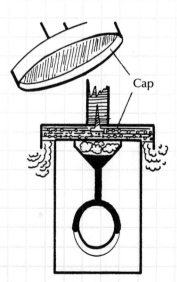

Another home remedy that is interesting

uses the same idea as the air pressure system.

It uses steam as formed by a wet pad applied to the top

when metal is melted in the sprue button.

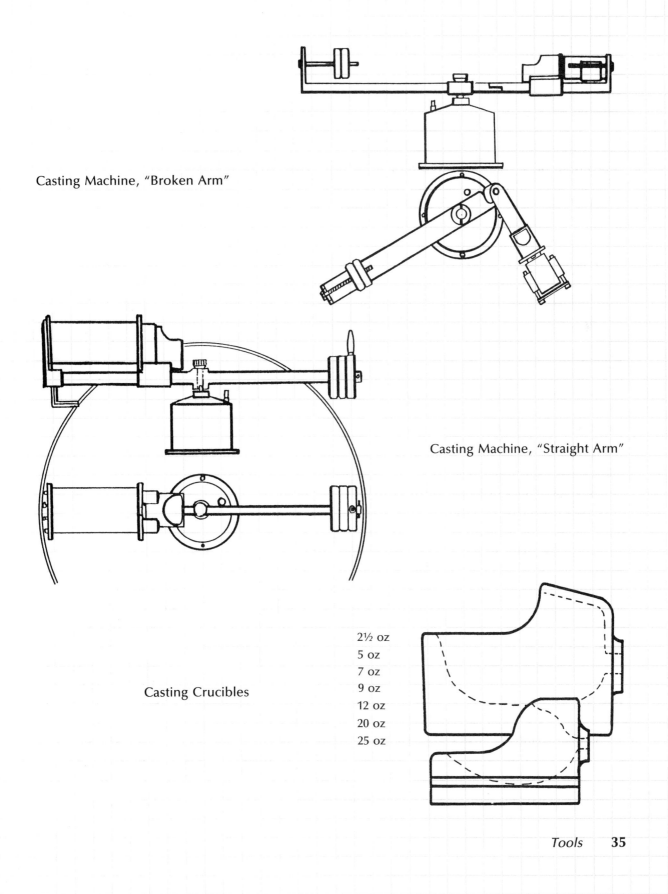

Casting Machine, "Broken Arm"

Casting Machine, "Straight Arm"

Casting Crucibles

2½ oz
5 oz
7 oz
9 oz
12 oz
20 oz
25 oz

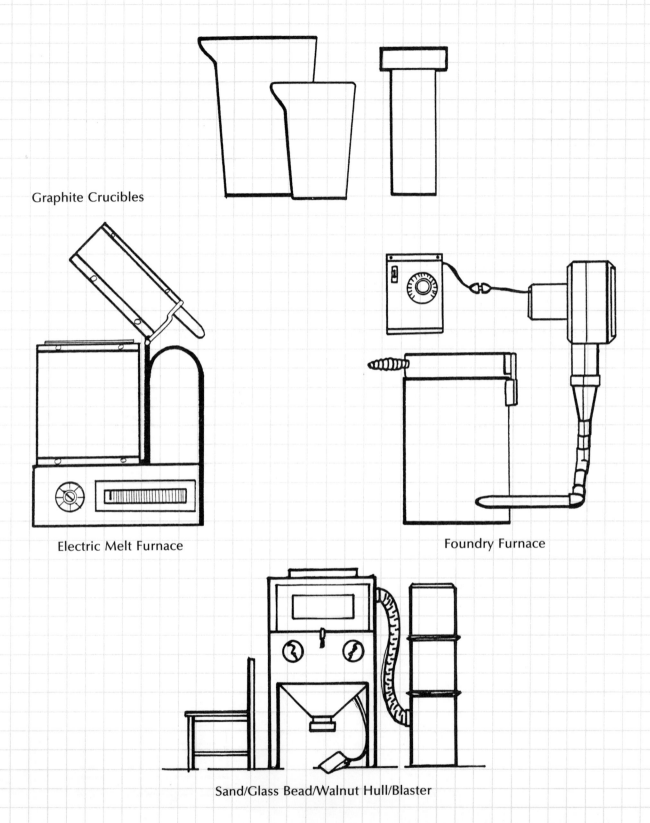

Graphite Crucibles

Electric Melt Furnace

Foundry Furnace

Sand/Glass Bead/Walnut Hull/Blaster

TOOLS FOR WAXING

Biology Teaser/Probe

A biology teaser/probe with a

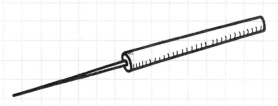

wood handle is the best.

It's O.K. with a plastic handle.

It is inexpensive.

You need to hammer one point into knife or spear edge.

It is handy to point the handle end with a knife or in the pencil sharpener.

To smooth the point and tip use extra fine sand paper.

The spear point is used hot to cut thin sheets of wax and wax wire.

The spear/knife edge is used to carve wax sheets and to pierce wax sheets.

It is also used to join sheet and wire wax.

It can be used to shape wire wax.

Knives

A knife can be used many ways.

A Biology solid metal scalpel with broad blade is my favorite.

An Exacto knife with broad blade is also good for cutting pink or green sheets.

A knife is good for cutting wax wire.

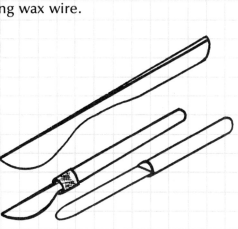

A knife is best for

   smoothing broad buildups and

   trimming wax shapes or edges.

Flat Metal Knife

   A palette knife or a cheap butter knife can be used to

   form broad areas of wax or

   smooth broad areas of wax.

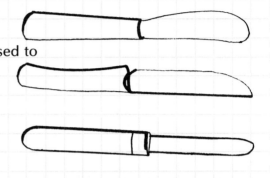

Trailing Tools

A trailing tool tip is

   blunt or round.

   Wax will position itself

   on the bottom of the tip

   for positive trailing control.

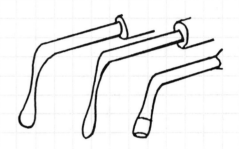

Useable dental waxing instruments are the

   P. K. Thomas wax placer #1 and

   P. K. Thomas wax placer #2.

   Healthco and Smith also make waxing tools.

   "George's California" trailing tool

   is one of the best.

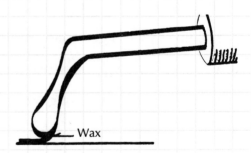

"Georges California" Trailing Tool

      Make your own

      in several sizes.

      Use brazing rod, silver wire or

      heavy coat hanger wire.

For wax trails of different thickness use:

8 gauge rod for a heavy trail,

10 gauge for a medium trail,

12 gauge for a fine trail,

16 gauge for an extra fine trail.

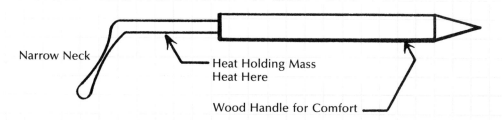

Narrow Neck

Heat Holding Mass
Heat Here

Wood Handle for Comfort

A narrow neck is hotter because it is thinner and draws wax to it and the tip. The wax trails off the bottom of the tip. As the thick body holds heat longer this enables the wax to flow smoother.

How to Make a "George's California" Trailing Tool.

Cut a 3-inch length of wire.

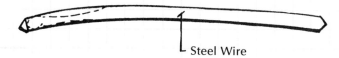

Steel Wire

Round one end with a file or emery cloth.

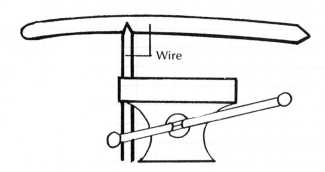

Wire

Point the other end to drive into wood handle.

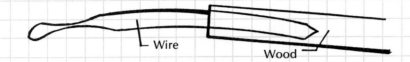

File into wire ½" above round end and shape to wasp waist.

Can thicken body to hold heat longer.

Add wire just after bend for ¾" to ⅞".

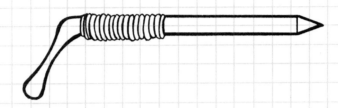

Solder wire coiled around body.

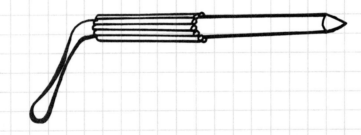

Solder cluster of parallel wires.

Drill hole into the end of handle 1" deep.

   Use a drill bit slightly smaller than wire diameter, or

   use a drill bit the same size as the wire.

To push wire into handle,

   put wire into vise, point up.

   Add a dab of glue to the point if you wish.

Put handle over point.

Join together by tapping the handle with mallet to seat the wire.

Clamp ¾″ to 1⅛″ of the round tip end in the vise.

Bend to a 50 degree angle.

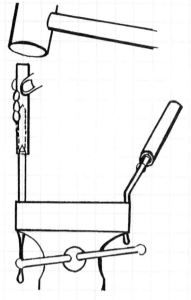

Heating Devices

To heat the hand held wax tools:

Use a candle,

an alcohol wick lamp or

a Bunsen burner with natural gas.

You can make your own natural gas burner.

Candle

The candle is a good heat source.

It is inexpensive

(one white emergency candle lasts about 4 hours).

The carbon darkening of the wax aids in seeing texture.

The carbon in wax will not affect or cause porosity if the burnout is proper (carbon

vaporizes during burnout).

Is easily available.

Is very portable.

Has a flame that is easily seen.

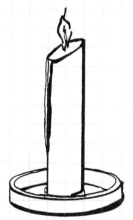

Alcohol Lamp

The alcohol lamp is a hot heat source.

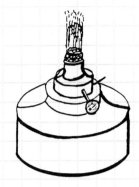

It is inexpensive to use

(burns about ⅓ cup of denatured alcohol per hour).

Is portable with care.

Creates no carbon.

Has adjustable flame

(flame is difficult to see in daylight or lamplight).

Bunsen Burner

The Bunsen burner is a hot heat source.

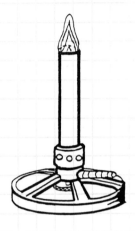

Uses natural or manufactured gas.

It has good flame adjustment.

The flame is easily seen.

Put it on a tilt base or

wax will drip down the burner tube and clog it.

No tool is an end in itself.

Use it for what it does best.

Then use another tool, if necessary, to

change or modify the object to your vision.

Make Your Own Gas Burner.

To make your own gas burner:

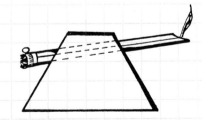

Use a ¼" copper tube.

Hammer the end closed.

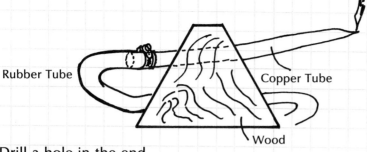

Rubber Tube   Copper Tube

Wood

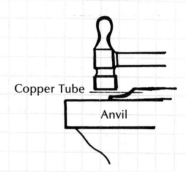

1/16" Drill or Finer

Drilled Hole

Copper Tube

Copper Tube

Anvil

Drill a hole in the end.

Drill a hole in a block of wood.

Mount the tube in the hole in the wood.

Clamp the copper to a length of

    standard laboratory gas hose.

The small hole in the copper will

    cause the gas flame to be long and thin,

    just right for brushing the wax smooth.

The hand held alcohol lamp with a

    plastic bottle base has a pipette attachment.

    Squeeze the bottle for a pinpoint brush flame.

    It is very good for smoothing wax.

    Use lots of little squeezes for best results

        in sustaining a brushing flame.

Electric Hand Held Wax Melter/Welder/Pen/Waxer

    Many different kinds of electric tools are on the market.

    Melt the wax with a heated electric controlled tip on a handle.

    Waxer controls the temperature of melting the wax and

    delivering the wax to the model for build up or trailing.

The Wax Gun

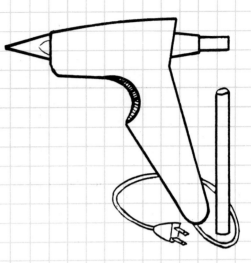

Has good wax flow control.

Is moderately priced.

Has a poor thickness selection

(16 ga to 12 ga).

Has a large nozzle and is built like a glue gun,

large and awkward.

It is great for wax wire creations

on cold water.

The gun uses wax rods 2" long × ½" diameter which

is lots of wax for long wires.

It can pull wire into the air, and

can layer up the wax on a mandrel.

All will be thick wax wire type construction,

which can be smoothed with another tool

for solid or shaped forms.

It uses 3 types of wax,

blue, green, and red; and

comes in a kit with documentation.

The Wax Pen With Reservoir

Comes with a many-temperature heat control.

It has excellent wax flow control,

and uses three different size tips.

Though it is the most expensive waxing tool, the

reservoir gives the tool a long

trailing or build up time.

It uses a positive wax flow control, and

is light weight.

The reservoir does make the balance awkward but

nothing you can't get used to.

The reservoir enables you to

use all types of wax.

Wax Pen/Welder/Waxers

All have multi-temperature heat control and

good wax flow control.

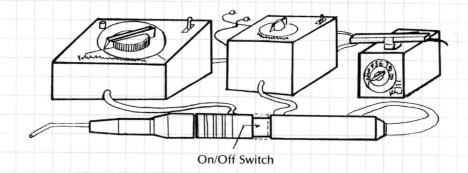

On/Off Switch

3 to 6 heating tips.

Only one for trailing build up that is

great for small to fine build up.

One broad tip for large lay up.

The tips change easily.

The pen is light and easy to use.

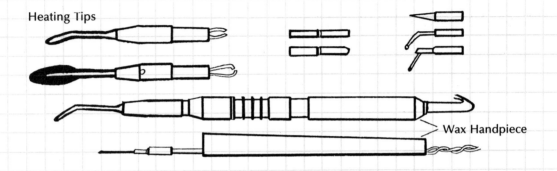

Heating Tips

Wax Handpiece

You need to touch wax to the tip and

then deposit as necessary.

There is excellent tip vision.

You can do anything with the waxer that

your handmade trailing tool will do, and

do it faster.

5

TORCHES FOR CASTING

Most shops use one of the six kinds of torches used for jewelry.

The natural gas and compressed air system is

used in many school shops for silver soldering;

but it is not hot enough for casting.

The hydrogen and oxygen torch is

used in professional shops for microsoldering.

It is very hot for very fast soldering of chain or ring bands.

The torch is not large enough for casting.

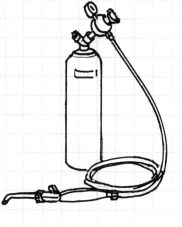

Acetylene, also known as Presto-Lite can be

used for heavy soldering.

It can be used for casting and is

used in many shops.

The gas has good heat range and has a

moderate cost per tank.

The tanks come in several sizes and

can be very portable.

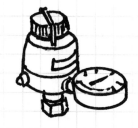

Presto-Lite
Tank, Gauge
and Hand Piece

The oxygen and acetylene combination is very hot and is

used for welding.

It can be used for casting but use a soft flame.

Care should be taken not to heat metal too fast or you

will burn metal and

change the alloy.

Oxygen and "L.P." (liquid propane) gas is moderately hot.

It is used for soldering and

used for casting.

It has an excellent temperature range and is

hot enough for pinpoint soldering.

Several sizes of tanks are available,

some small enough to be portable.

The oxygen and natural gas combination is

the same as oxygen and liquid propane,

except it is not portable.

It is the cheapest gas combination

if you have the gas in the building.

Lighting the Acetylene Torch

To light the acetylene torch,

first light a match and

hold it near the tip.

Turn the little knurled knob on the handpiece

one turn clockwise (away from you) and pop! It's lit!

The flame only has two adjustments, low and high.

To turn the torch off, turn the little knob on the handpiece

counterclockwise (toward you) and pop! It's off!

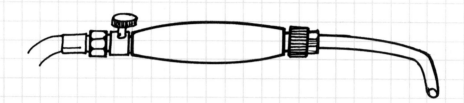

If you are the last person to use the torch

during this casting series,

you are to shut it down.

Turn the long rusty handle clockwise

closing the valve firmly.

Turn open the little knob on the torch.

Watch the gauges go down to the hiss of

released gas from the torch.

When both gauges read "zero" close valve on the torch and

turn the handle between the gauges so it screws out.

Turn two or three times.

That's it!

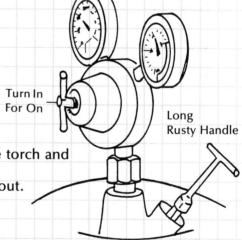

Turn In
For On

Long
Rusty Handle

Lighting The Acetylene Torch

Lighting the torch that

uses oxygen and natural gas.

The red hose is always for gas.

The green hose is always for oxygen.

If the knobs on your torch aren't marked

you can trace the hose to the gas knob.

Light your match or

use the spark lighter.

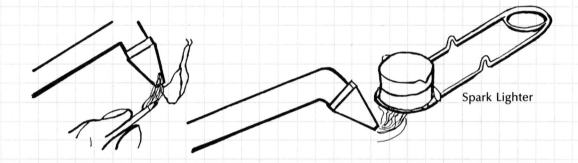

Spark Lighter

Hold the lit match or

sparking spark lighter over the tip.

Turn the gas knob just barely one clockwise turn.

The gas will ignite and

the torch will be lit.

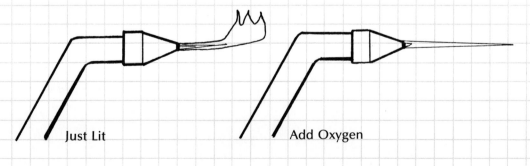

Just Lit   Add Oxygen

Adjust the torch to the hottest flame by

turning on more gas.

Add more oxygen slowly,

until the flame is pointy and blue.

Add more gas.

Then add more oxygen

until you get a long hard flame.

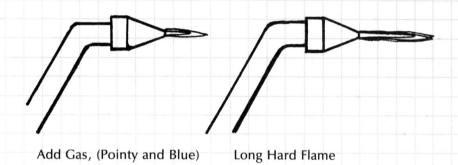

Add Gas, (Pointy and Blue)   Long Hard Flame

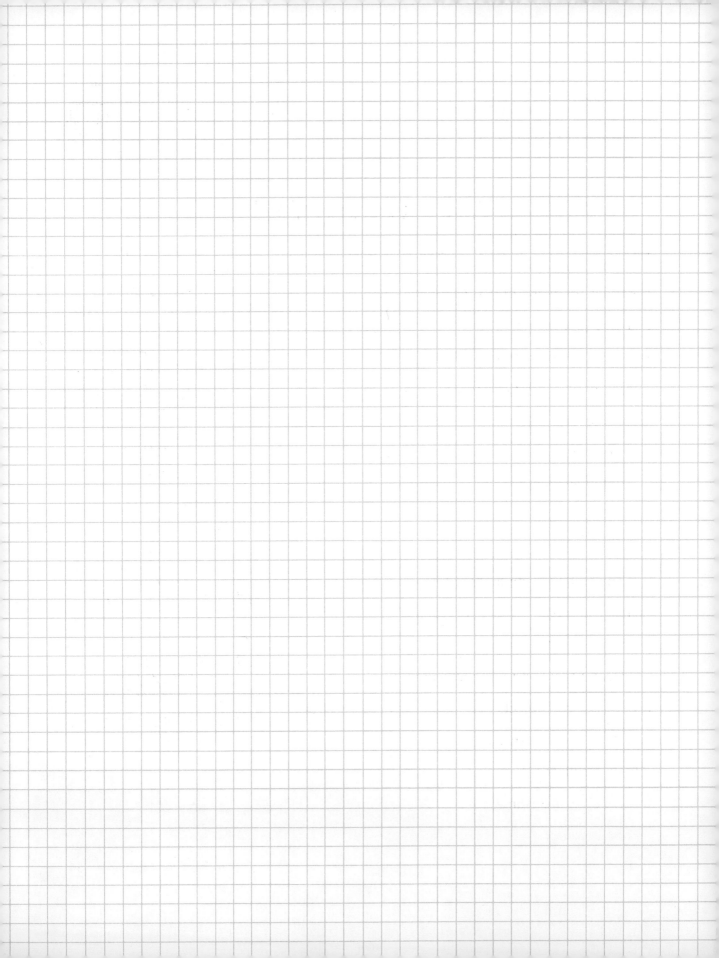

6

WAX TECHNIQUES

Texture is the name of the game with wax.

Softened wax will accept any pressed image.

There are many every day objects

    that can be used in a repeat to make a pattern.

    For example:

        Paper clips.

        Bobby pins.

        Safety pins.

        Wrapped wire.

        The metal serrations on pencils.

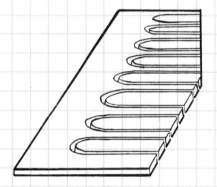

    Heat the object and press onto/into wax.

        Wipe the object clean.

        Heat it again and press into the wax.

There are many objects that can be pressed into wax.

You can use them to:

    Form a collage.

    Form an embellishment.

    Form a border.

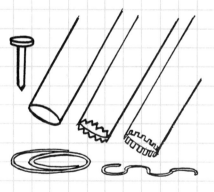

You can use the following to press into the wax.

An etching plate.

A wood cut.

A linoleum cut.

Antique metal patterns.

Spoon patterns can be pressed to wax.

To prevent wax from sticking to an object,

coat the object with a light oil.

You can also coat the object with detergent,

(just a thin coat will do).

You can use plastic wrap

on flat or slightly curved forms.

There are many objects/forms that wax can be formed over.

Form over

dapping dies,

wood forms,

plastic forms, or

metal.

Coat the object with a light oil, or

thinly coat object with detergent.

To use plastic wrap,

warm the wax to soften and then

press over the object.

Let it cool, and remove carefully.

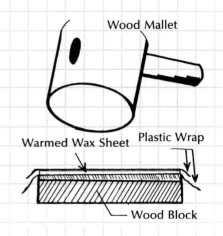

Wood Mallet

Warmed Wax Sheet   Plastic Wrap

Wood Block

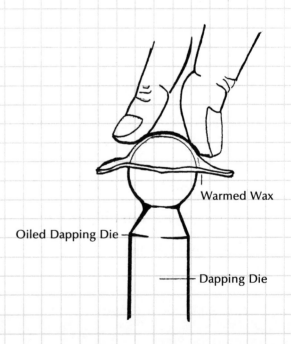

Warmed Wax

Oiled Dapping Die

Dapping Die

WAX SHEET FABRICATION

When you want to join wax edge to edge,

first warm the wax.

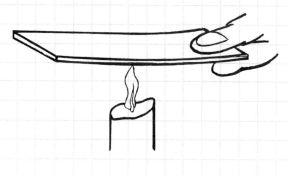

Immediately place/press the wax into place.

Next, warm the probe in a flame.

Then cut a bit of blue and

melt it on the probe.

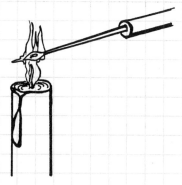

Touch the tool to the joint,

moving the tool along the joint.

Repeat until the joint is filled.

Turn the form over and

fill the joint on other side.

To join a band for a ring,

cut a strip of pink wax with a warm knife

to ring size.

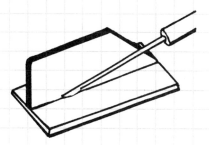

Warm the strip to make it flexible and

wrap it around the mandrel.

Size the ring a quarter size smaller than you need.

The filing and sanding done to finish the inside

will bring the band back to size.

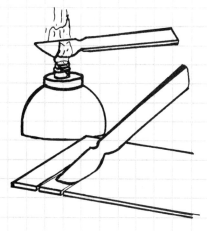

It is always easier to enlarge a band

than to make it smaller.

To join the ends together,

   use the probe and bits

   to build up a hump.

   Smooth it with a heated knife.

   Now trim and shape the band with a heated knife.

   Texture the band at this time if you wish,

   with a heated metal shape such as

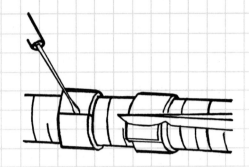

      a round nail,

      a shaped nail,

      a bobby pin, or

      any appropriate object.

To add a plate to a plate,

   warm the top plate to about 100° F

      under a light bulb,

      over a flame or

      in warm water.

   Press the plate into place

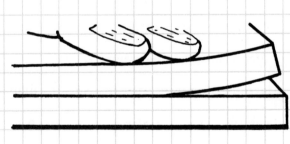

      gently but firmly; and

      watch out for fingerprints.

   Use the heat probe to seal all edges all the way around.

   If you don't seal the edges,

   investment will get in between and

   will be broken off during the casting

   by the incoming metal, causing large pits.

The Finished Edges of Wax Sheet

To crisp and finish the edges of wax sheet,

first stroke it with a heated, broad knife.

Then file it with a coarse sand paper or

any kind of rough paper.

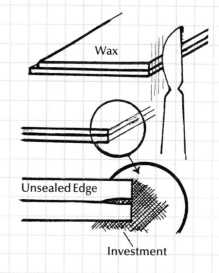

To polish the wax with paper,

wrap a square of paper around a hard object such as a

dowel rod and stroke the wax with the paper.

You can also tape the paper to a desk surface and

stroke the wax on the paper.

To soften the edges of the wax sheet,

stroke edge with a flame.

Continual stroking will cause

the wax to draw into itself.

The cause is a heavy, smooth frame-like border/edge.

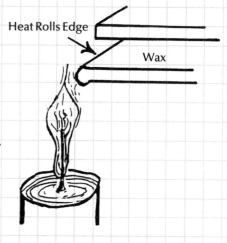

If you wish to pierce the sheet,

heat the probe to smoking and

push through the sheet.

Withdraw the probe and

blow at the hole with a sharp puff.

This has to be done quickly while the wax is still melted.

This technique is

great for making holes, great for making negative lines, and

great for making small negative shapes.

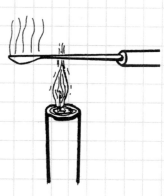

Carving a Shallow Relief Into the Wax Sheet

First warm the knife edge probe.

Then draw/make shallow cuts in the wax

to form shapes.

Hold the knife probe at an angle and

cut a wide tapered groove

around the entire shape.

Now hold the knife as flat as possible

to make a series of probing cuts.

Next peel the wax out of the cut shape.

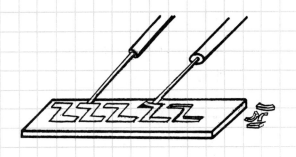

Joining Wire to Wire

The basic joining of wire to wire or wire to plate.

Hold the wire very close but

not touching the joining site.

Heat the probe smoking hot.

Touch the probe to the end of the wax wire.

Quickly touch the wire to the joining site.

Just touch and the wax will flow and join.

When touching melted wax to wax,

don't push into the site

unless you want a

concave ring around the

wire at the point of touching.

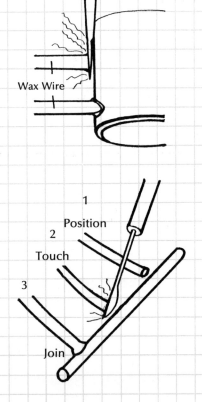

Wax Wire

1
Position

2
Touch

3

Join

Blow at the wax to cool and

cut the wax to length with the probe.

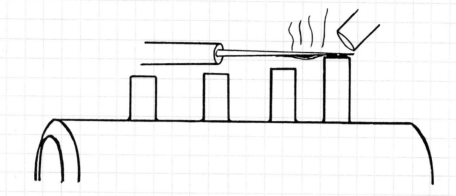

You can touch up the wax joint if necessary,

using melted wax on a probe.

Adjust angle of wire to desired position.

Practice on scrap.

You'll catch on quickly.

Add wax until even or

add wax until a bump is formed.

A bump can be removed

    with a file or

    with sand paper.

    See the wax finishing page (74).

Joined wire can be formed into objects after constructing.

  Warm the wax to 30° F to 120° F

    under a light bulb, or

    dip in warm water.

Wire forms can be built over objects.

Don't forget to warm the wire first.

Cold wire is brittle.

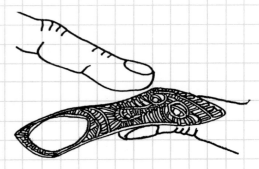

Join and press the warmed wax into place.

The wire's shape can be changed easily.

Changing the shape of the wax will increase the visual variety.

Changing the shape of the wax will develop crisp consistency.

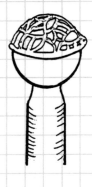

Changing the shape of the wax will develop textural consistency.

You can taper the wax.

Stroke the wax from the desired

thin to the thick with

a heated, but not smoking probe.

Blow gently at the probe as

you get toward the thick end.

If you wish to flatten one side of the round wire

stroke the length of wire

with a heated probe.

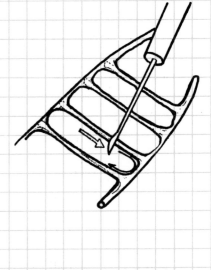

Be sure to wipe the probe clean

after each stroke.

If you wish to thicken a wire,

pick up a wax nugget with the probe.

Heat the probe behind the wax nugget.

The melted wax, not the probe

should touch the wire.

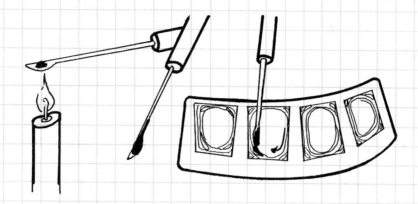

You will need to blow gently

to freeze the wax in its shape

as the probe is moving.

When you want to make pseudo granulation

take a wire

hold the end over the flame.

The wax will draw up into

a ball when it melts.

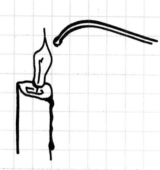

Wait a second, then

touch the ball

to the wax sheet or wire.

The ball will stick.

If you touch the ball to the wax

too soon it will blob.

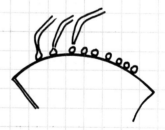

If you touch the ball to the wax

too late the ball won't stick.

The same wax wire will make

the same size ball time after time.

The size of the ball

is controlled by

the size of the wax wire.

The larger diameter of wax wire

the larger the ball.

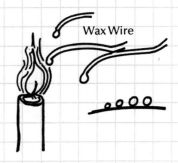
Wax Wire

This technique is tricky but not difficult.

Touch the ball too soon and

the wax will blob.

Touch the ball too late and

it won't stick.

Practice.

Practice.

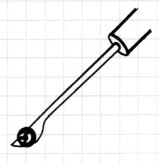

Trailing

Trailing is the building up of wax in thin layers.

The success is in the tool.

With the regular probe or needle,

the wax won't go to the very tip.

The side of a probe

or needle eye can be used for

some trailing techniques.

The best, most versatile shape

for a trailing tool is blunt or rounded.

The wax will coat the bottom of the tool,

putting the wax in position for trailing.

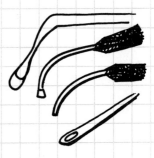

The wax on the end of the tool

just barely touches the point where you wish to start.

Slowly, move the tool in the desired direction.

Gently blow at the tool to

freeze the wax as you move the tool.

 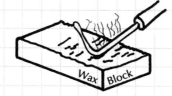 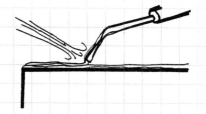

Trailing within wire shapes is a logical way to start a form.

Join 18 gauge wax wire to a desired shape.

Trail the wax inside the shape.

This technique is good for container forms.

Do several forms to fit together. Assemble them after casting.

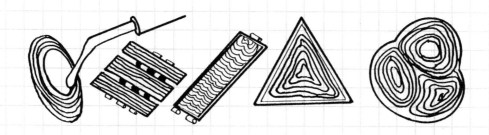

You can trail on wax wire or wax sheet,

  build up wall forms or

  small towers

    to set stones.

Trailing in the air is exciting to do.

  As you're pulling your trail,

  lift the tool in the air

  blowing as you lift.

  You can trail about an inch

  of wax at a time.

  Once you catch on,

  air trails are great.

There is a feeling of freedom that's neat.

After your first air pull,

strengthen the base with more wax

before the next pull.

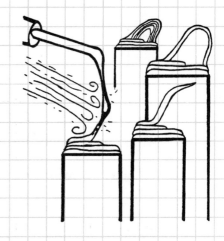

When you add length in the air

you'll find it easy to change direction.

Some folks find it harder to trail straight.

In any case, be gentle,

the trailed wax is fragile.

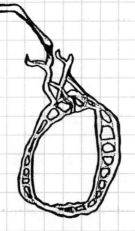

Laying On Wax

Laying on wax is a valuable skill.

Often you need to build up a form in specific areas.

To do this

    heat nuggets of wax on a knife

      to get a broad stroke.

    Heat nuggets of wax on spoon tool,

    apply in a large dribble

      for a thick stroke.

  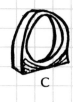

A   B   C

    Heat nuggets of wax on a knife probe

      for a thin stroke.

    It is easy to lay down a tear drop.

    It is harder to lay down a broad flat area.

    Try laying down a series of overlapping tear drops or blobs,

      then smooth them with a hot knife blade.

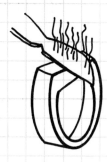

Dipping

When dipping objects in wax for workable forms to modify,

melting the wax is critical to this technique.

A double boiler is best.

Put wax in a pan over

a pan filled with water.

Heat on a stove, or

on a hot plate, or

over a Bunsen burner.

   (The Bunsen burner is less safe

   but okay if you are careful.)

You can melt the wax in a pan in the oven safely.

Be sure to set the oven at the melting point of the wax.

Wax can explode if overheated.

Smoking wax is very close to

its igniting point.

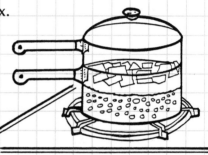

It is very dangerous to melt wax

in a pan directly over a heat source.

It is so easy to overheat and explode.

Don't take the chance of being severely burned.

Use the double boiler method.

It is no more trouble to do it safely.

Once the wax is melted dip an oiled mandrel into the wax.

You can spoon wax onto the oiled mandrel.

Dip several to many times.

To build up a thickness,

let wax or mandrel cool before dipping again.

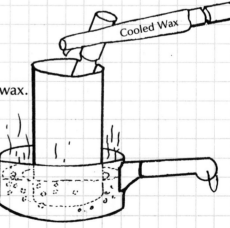

Cooled Wax

Heat the end of the mandrel to slide the wax off.

You cut the wax with a wire.

Just wrap the wire around

the wax and saw down to the mandrel.

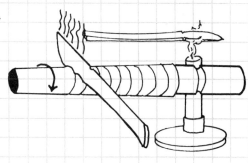

You can cut the wax with a hot knife.

Cut several sections of the wax

and remove by heating the mandrel

until the wax starts to melt.

Then slide the wax off

and separate with

a hot knife or thin wire.

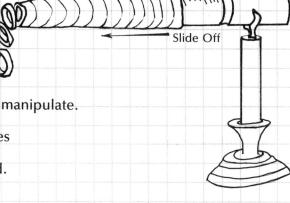

Slide Off

You can dip other materials that are easy to manipulate.

Dip a good rag paper several to many times

    to build up the thickness of wax desired.

Dip a tissue.

    Use paper.

    Kleenex, Puffs, etc., for dipping.

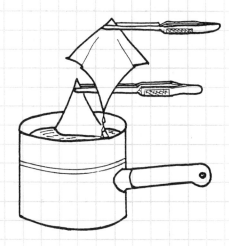

You can dip some types of cloth.

    Cotton or linen will burn clean.

    Dip once to maintain texture.

Cut the paper, tissues, cloth or

warmed wax with heated scissors.

Waxed cloth or paper can be shaped into

crisp hard forms that are easily formed and easily added to.

Dripping

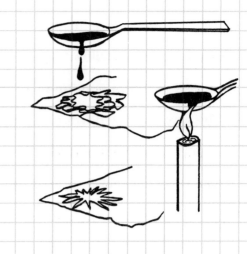

Dripping is another technique to explore.

    Drip wax into cold water.

    Drip wax onto oiled aluminum foil.

    This creates splatter forms.

    Use a spoon to drip the wax.

    Different wax patterns can

    be formed by overlapping the spatters

    and by changing the height

    of the spoon while dripping.

Pouring

You can pour wax directly from a small pan.

    Different diameter wax patterns can

    be formed by changing the

    height and thickness of the wax stream

      and the amount of wax poured.

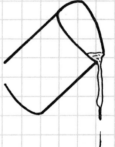

    Try pouring wax from a spoon or

    pour wax from a metal tube.

Dripping and pouring rarely are ends in themselves.

Their parts, their bits and pieces are interesting.

    They are good to build on or

    to be used as accessories or

    parts to other jewelry pieces.

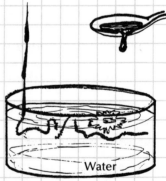

Water

Plastic

Plastic can be an interesting parts library for casting.

Not all plastics are good to use for casting.

Wax won't stick to some,

making modification difficult.

Some won't burn out clean.

The best plastics to use are those used in plastic model kits.

The tanks, cars, planes, animals, and plastic flowers are all castable part by part.

Railroad gauge scale people,

animals, and other accessories

are good too, if unpainted.

The plastic parts usually need to be cleaned up before use.

You will need to file or shave edge flashing,

as well as sprue marks and parting lines.

Use an engraver to crisp details

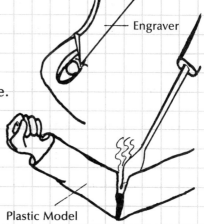

Engraver

Plastic Model

to desired sharpness.

You can cut with a sharp knife,

or saw with a jewelers saw.

Add details or patterns with wax, and

use wax for joining parts together.

Styrofoam is a usable plastic for casting.

You will need to seal its very rough surface with wax.

All plastics need a longer burn out.

Add 1 hour to the red soak time (see page 120).

Organic Materials

Organic materials are design possibilities for casting.

Most organic materials can be cast.

The leaves, flower petals,

dried weeds, dried flowers,

insects, popcorn, and

breakfast food can be cast into metal.

The only limitation is will it burn out completely.

Sea shells and

teeth will not burn out completely.

Thick wood (10 gauge or thicker) will not burn out completely.

The material must be totally consumed

during the burn out.

See page 119 for burn out information.

Loose ash can be removed

after normal burn out.

Do not cast the flask until the ash is removed.

Let the flask cool.

When the flask is cold

pour mercury into the cavity of the mold.

The mercury will break up the ash

and the ash will float to the surface.

Pour mercury out.

Repeat until there is no sign of ash, then heat to 400° F and cast.

Any organic materials that dissolve in water

    need a protective coating.

      Pasta,

      popcorn,

      bread,

      sugar, and

      corn flakes, for example,

    need to have their surfaces sealed.

    You can dip the mold in wax and

    shake the excess wax off.

    You can paint the objects with lacquer or

    dip in lacquer and shake off the excess.

    Continue with normal casting procedures.

Thin organic materials such as

    insect wings,

    insect leg and body joints,

    flower petals, and

    leaves need thickening with wax.

    Try adding wax to the object with a probe.

    Add wax to the object with a trailing tool.

    Dip the object in wax and

    shake excess wax off.

    Paint the object with lacquer or

    dip in lacquer and shake excess wax off.

Carving

Carving wax is a popular model-making technique.

All wax can be carved.

The best carving wax is hard yet flexible

but not brittle.

The blue is good.

Yellow is good.

Red is good.

Purple is good.

Use the wax for dipping and

then carve the form.

Use the wax for build up and

then carve the form.

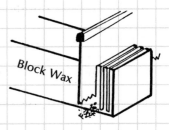

Block Wax

You can pour the wax into sheets on soaped glass.

Remove from the surface, wash

and cut to shape.

Carve the wax into forms.

Heat the wax form to soften and

wrap or twist into forms.

Melt and cast the wax into blocks.

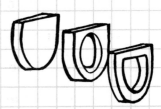

Carvex is a brand name for a wax made just for carving.

You can saw off a chunk of wax or

slice pieces for use.

Drill holes in the pieces for rings and then carve as you wish.

You can texture the wax model

with a file or

with sand paper.

You can impress patterns into the model

using heated metal forms.

Make your own "branding irons"

with copper or brass or

use found objects.

Tools used for carving are

a sharp knife, or

an *Exacto* blade.

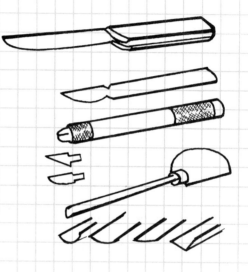

Shave the wax rather than cut chunks.

Linoleum carving tools or

wood block carving tools,

are excellent to use on wax.

When you use the tools, scrape and pare the wax.

Use shallow, not coarse, cuts into the wax.

A jewelers saw with a coarse blade cuts wax easily.

Wax cutting burrs, made for use in

a flexible shaft machine, come

in a variety of shapes.

You can use them in a drill press.

You can use them by twisting them by hand.

FINISHING THE WAX

Most of the time it is easier to work the wax than the metal.

You need to work the wax to near perfection.

Scratches, gouges or hollows

need to be filled now.

Stroke with extra fine sandpaper or a paper towel around

a probe handle,

a wood dowel rod or

a file.

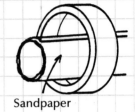

Sandpaper

If you need to identify holes that need to be filled,

polish the wax and

the areas that need to be filled will show.

To polish use paper towels

wrapped around a shaped piece of wood or

a file and

stroke gently.

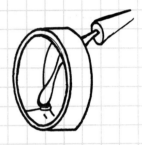

Wet cotton is good to polish with.

Use cotton swabs or

spin cotton on a burned wooden kitchen match.

Then put in a flexible shaft machine,

hand piece and touch wax gently

with flexible shaft at low speed.

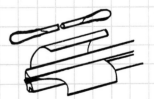

The match trick can get into almost any area

you wish to polish.

STONE SETTING

The principle behind designing and making a setting for a stone is quite simple. Basically, a "set" is made to prevent the stone from moving; to hold it rigidly in place.

A stone can move only four ways.

It can move up and down or

back and forth.

The stone must have a seat, a place to rest upon.

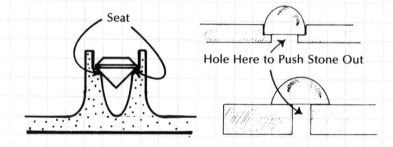

The set must have contact points that will push against the stone to hold it to its seat.

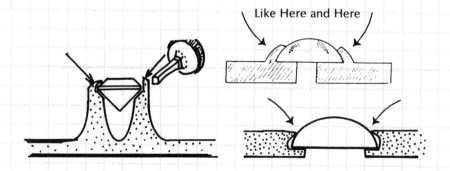

There are only two main types of holding techniques to hold a stone in place.

One is the contact point that goes along the edge of a stone.

It is pushed against the stone to hold it firm.

It is called a bezel.

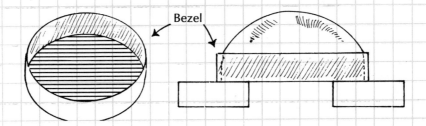

The second type has contact points that are placed at intervals to prevent the stone from moving.

They are called prongs.

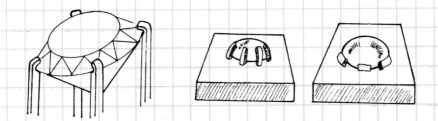

A round stone needs at least three prongs.

More prongs can be used, but at least three are necessary so the stone cannot move.

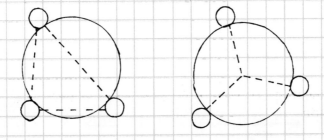

A rectangular shaped stone must have at least four contact points, sometimes six to hold the stone in place.

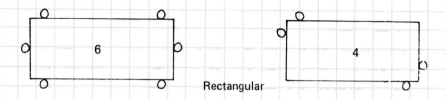

Rectangular

Eight contact points are the safest to hold the stone.

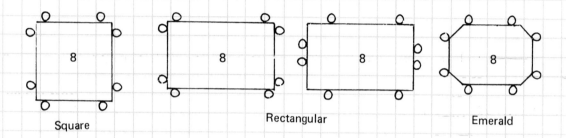

Square   Rectangular   Emerald

The only exception is the emerald shaped gem stones.

Traditionally, with this cut of gem, four points are used on the corner flats and are considered safe.

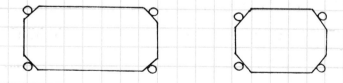

A stone must also have these contact points arranged in such a way so the stone cannot move from side to side.

An oval or marque-shaped stone must have at least four contact points to hold the gem secure.

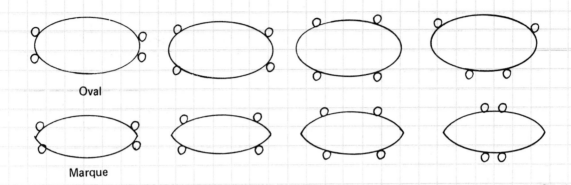

Oval

Marque

More contact points can be used but four is the minimum.

Use the prongs as a pattern or decorative element, but use at least four to really hold the gem secure.

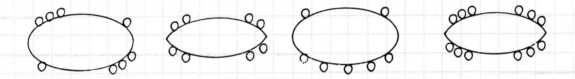

A square or an emerald-shaped stone must have *at least* four, sometimes six contact points to hold the gem.

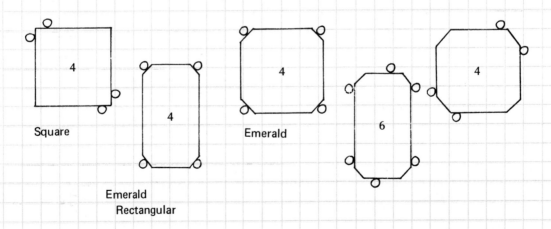

Square

Emerald
Rectangular

Emerald

There are many different shapes of stones.

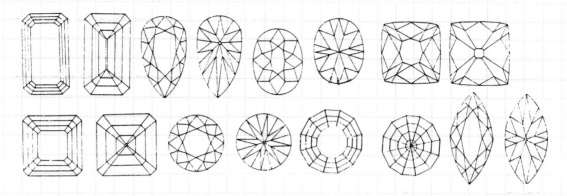

The names of the parts of gems are:

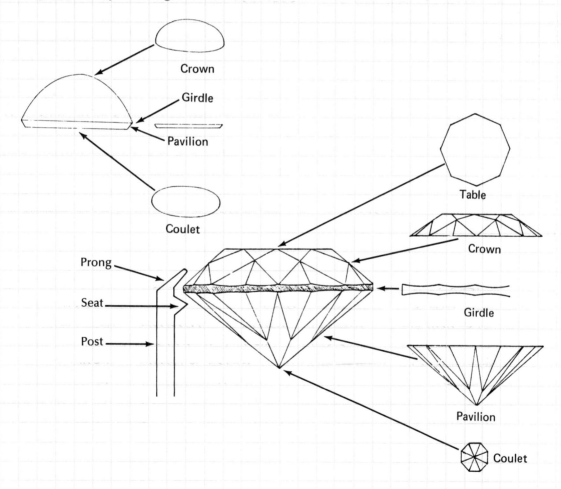

Crown

Girdle

Pavilion

Coulet

Prong

Seat

Post

Table

Crown

Girdle

Pavilion

Coulet

MOUNTS

The Crown Mount

Different gem holding arrangements are called mounts.

The crown mount, the flat oval mount and the three post mount are just a few mount designs available for the artist to use.

Wrap a wax wire around the stone on the pavilion next to the girdle.

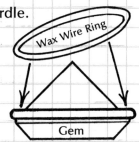

Use green wax wire, or use blue wax wire.

Use round-shaped wax wire.

Use square-shaped wax wire.

Use triangular-shaped wax wire.

Use a gauge of wax appropriate to the gem.

You can use 16, 18, 20 or 22 gauge.

The larger gauge for the larger stone.

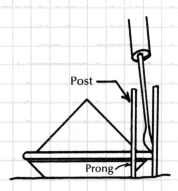

Measure the wax wire

by wrapping it around the gem just below the girdle.

Cut and join the wax wire to make a complete seat.

Rest the gem on its table.

Place seat on the gem just below the girdle.

Add prongs and posts to the gem as desired.

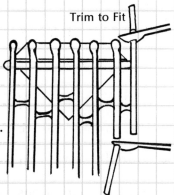

Adding wax wires joining the posts,

adds to the strength of the design.

The joining can be used as a pattern or as added decoration.

It is best to trim the prongs to their minimum length.

The minimum length being less than 30% of the crown face.

Warm and bend the prongs in place by

pushing with the handle of a probe.

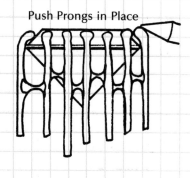

Push Prongs in Place

Trim the post to a length needed

to fit the body of the jewelry piece.

You can trim the seat wire to a minimum.

If you plan on casting the gem in place,

remember the statement:

"The least amount of metal (i.e., wax)

that touches the stone the better off you are."

You can remove the gem from the mount before casting.

Dip the wax in warm water to soften it.

Gently push or tap the coulet of the gem

to remove it from its setting.

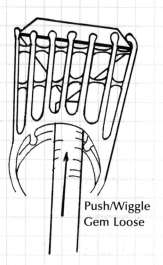

Push/Wiggle
Gem Loose

Be careful not to distort the wax

after removing the stone, or

the set will have to be readjusted to fit the stone.

To cast or not to cast the stone in place

is a question only you can answer.

The important things to consider are: Can you afford to lose the stone?

Can the stone be easily set after casting?

After casting can you clean and finish the metal around the stone?

Is the stone safe to cast?

Refer to the section on gems and casting of gems

for more suggestions about casting in place.

The Flat Oval Mount

The flat oval mount is used for smaller gems.

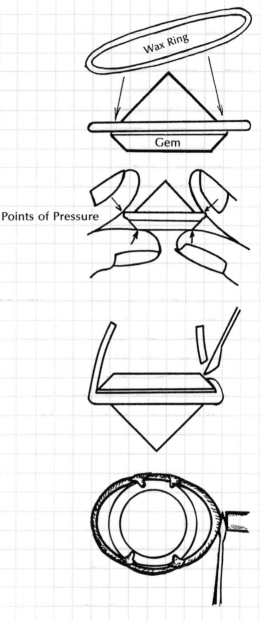

Make a circle with the wax wire

one-third larger than the stone.

Use blue wax wire or

use green wax wire in 18 or 20 gauge.

Round wax wire works best

as the base for this mount.

Wrap the wax wire around something to size,

such as a pencil or

a mandrel, to make a wax circle.

Pinch the wax circle to make an oval that

the pavilion of the stone can rest on.

Press the wax to the stone

at areas of contact near the circle.

Turn over the stone with wax pressed in place.

Add prongs and posts.

Use 18, 20, or 22 gauge round wax wire.

Trim the prongs to within

one-half to one-third the width of the crown.

Use this mount as a single in a band or

in clusters.

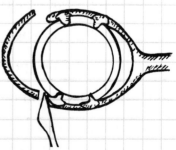

Use it vertically, horizontally or

as a dangle.

The Three Post Mount

The three post mount is a very traditional mount.

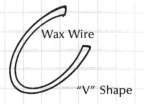

Wax Wire

Use this mount for small to

medium-sized stones

that stick up

rather than lay flat.

"V" Shape

Use the green or blue wax wire.

Use round wax wire,

square wax wire, or

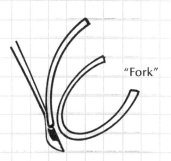

"Fork"

triangular wax wire.

Cut a short length of wax wire and

bend it into a "V" shape.

Add another wax wire to the "V"

to make a "fork."

"Fork" With Stem

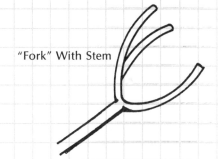

Add a wax stem to the bottom of the "fork":

Fill in the bottom and stem of the "fork"

to make the joints strong.

Press Prongs in Place

Hold the "mount" between the thumb and two fingers.

Spread the three prongs equally.

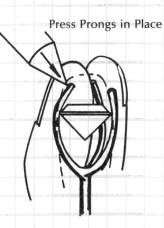

Drop the stone in place.

Align it the way you want it.

Gently but firmly push the stone in place so

your fingers and thumb can hold it.

Push the prongs against the stone.

Remove the set from your fingers.

Hold the mount upside down to trim the prongs

   to a minimum length.

Add a seat to each post

   with a probe and melted wax.

Make sure that all prongs are against the stone.

Four prong mounts can be done the same way.

   Use your thumb and three fingers.

   Join two "V's" together.

   The procedure is the same as for the three prong mount.

   You can use with or without a stem.

   Use the mount vertically,

      horizontally,

      obliquely or

      clustered.

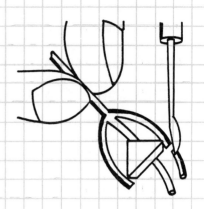

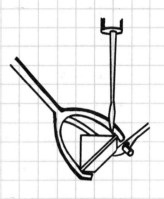

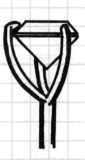

Cabochon Set

The Bezel Mount

Several Variations for Wax

Use these techniques for faceted or cabochon gems.

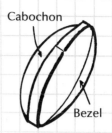

Cabochon

Bezel

A flat sheet strip is used for the bezel wall.

Use 24 or 26 gauge wax and

use the pink or green sheets of wax.

Warm the wax and cut it with a knife and a straight edge.

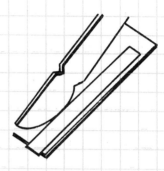

It will cut with scissors too.

Measure your stone circumference

with a strip of paper or masking tape.

Place the strip flat on a table.

Place the wax sheet over the cut measured length.

Cut the wax to length and width.

Join the ends to form the bezel.

The fit should be slightly loose,

rather than tight.

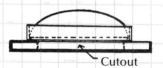

Cutout

This will aid you in removing the stone

before casting if you wish.

Place the bezel and the stone on a wax sheet.

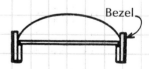

Bezel

Mark points next to wax bezel

all the way around it.

Put the stone and the bezel to one side.

Cut out the shape of the bezel to the outside of the bezel, or just inside the bezel.

Your choice!

If you cut to the outside of the bezel,

    turn it over and

    add the seat tabs to the bottom.

If you cut on the inside of the bezel

    the part you leave is the seat.

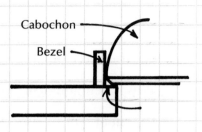

You can make it decorative by

    cutting the center out in a pattern or

    a shape.

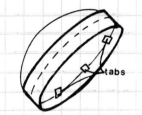

Position the bezel in place again and

    join it to the main body with a probe and melted wax.

If you add decoration to the bezel,

    don't interfere with the burnishing,

    that is, bending the bezel to the stone.

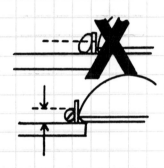

Another Variation of the Theme

To point out that there usually (or almost always) is another way to do everything, here is another variation of the bezel mount theme.

Make a flat sheet strip.

    Use the 22 or 24 gauge

    pink or green sheet wax.

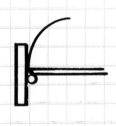

Warm the wax and

    cut with a knife and a straight edge.

    You can cut the warm wax with scissors if you wish.

    Measure the wax to the stone.

    Join the ends of the wire together.

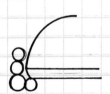

Make the joint clean, smooth, and

fit it to the stone.

Now make a wire ring to fit inside the bezel.

Use 20 or 22 gauge wax wire.

Add the wire ring to the bezel against the pavilion of stone.

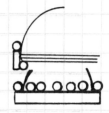

Join the wax ring to the wax bezel

with heat, to make the seat.

Don't interfer with the burnishing of the bezel

with your design.

More Variations of the Theme

Here are two or more additional variations of the bezel mount.

Make a wire ring to fit

around the girdle of a stone.

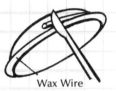

Wax Wire

Remove from the stone and

trail on the ring to start a bezel.

Trail wax in either direction.

Trail from the stone down

to the main body.

Trail from the stone base up.

The holding bezel

does not have to be straight.

It can go in waves or

scallops or

crown points.

You know that any change makes a variation.

Use round wax wire of

16 or 18 gauge blue wax.

Choose a heavier gauge if the stone is large.

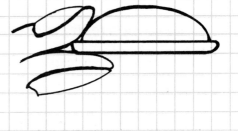

Fit the wax wire ring to the girdle of the stone.

Add prongs as the seat.

They can be loops,

diamond shaped or

petal shaped.

Press the wax ring to make sure it

goes beyond the girdle just a bit.

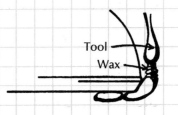

Tool

Wax

Now, trail a wax rim onto the wire for the bezel.

Reminders:

Bezels only need to be high enough to hold the stone.

Make sure you can push and burnish the bezel into place.

A bezel does not have to be straight or continuous.

It just has to stop the stone from falling out.

PRONGS

Flat Prongs

Flat prongs can look like fingers or claws.

The wax sheet can be cut into prong forms

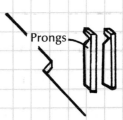

Prongs

notched to hold a stone.

This time use 12, 14 or 16 gauge sheet wax.

When cut, fasten one prong in place with melted wax.

Then position the others

in relationship with the stone.

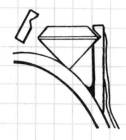

This technique works nicely on uneven surfaces.

Shaped Wire Prongs

Shaped wire prongs are the most versatile of the variations.

Wax wire can be cut and

built up or

trailed into prong forms.

Use round wax wire,

square wax wire or

triangular wax wire

for the base of the prong/post form.

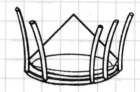

Notch the wire to hold the stone.

Fasten one or more of the prongs in place.

Position the other post and prongs

in relationship to the stone.

Tack them all in place and

put the stone in the mount.

Adjust the prongs to fit the stone and

fasten prongs in place with a hot probe and wax.

Flair the base for strength.

Join to each other with cross bars for strength.

CASTING GEMS IN PLACE

Leave the gem in the wax and

    put it through the casting procedure.

The main advantage is to

    open up design possibilities.

You can set stones where you couldn't before.

    You can set stones in hidden settings and

        in lace-like settings.

    Casting in place saves time,

        the set is tighter.

        You don't need to support gems during metal prong pushing,

        as the prongs are set in place before casting.

    The main disadvantage is that it is a gamble.

        You can't cast all stones.

        Of those stones you can cast

        you still can lose stones.

    Cast-in-place stones complicate cleanup and finishing.

        You cannot use a bright dip.

        You cannot use the butler finish.

    The gem is subjected to thermal shock.

        The gem will go through extreme expansion and extreme contraction,

        by the heating and cooling of it during burn out.

        The greatest risks are during the introduction of metal and

        during the cooling of the flask.

You can minimize thermal shock by

insulating the gem from the metal

as much as possible.

You can heat the invested flask to its upper temperature tolerance

closer to the temperature of the incoming metal.

You can allow the metal and flask to cool slowly.

Rule # 1 With an 80% success rate for natural gems and a 95% success rate for synthetic gems, *don't gamble unless you can afford to lose.*

Rule # 2 Always have a duplicate stone handy in case of loss.

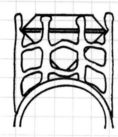

Rule # 3 The least amount of metal/wax that touches the stone the better off you are.

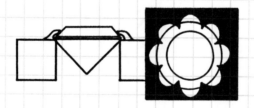

Rule # 4 Keep the prong and seat contact at a minimum. Use as many prongs and seats as you want, but to keep contact to a minimum, make the seats and prongs narrow.

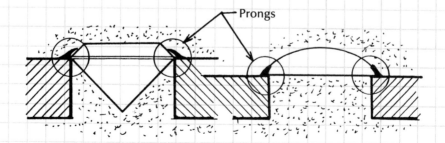

Prongs

Rule # 5 Keep space around, above and underneath the girdle open for investment to grab and hold the gem when the wax melts away.

Rule # 6 Keep space around the table and crown open for investment to hold the gem during burn out or during casting when there is no wax to hold the stone.

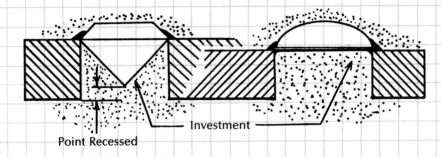

Point Recessed — Investment —

Rule # 7 Keep the space around the coulet and pavilion open for investment to hold the gem during burn out or during casting when the wax has melted away.

Rule # 8 Large stones are best set after casting.

Rule # 9 Bezels that encircle the stone are dangerous. When metal cools, it contracts, putting pressure on the stone possibly causing fractures. Encirclement can develop maximum thermal shock which results in internal crazing or fracturing fracturing of the gem.

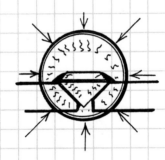

Rule #10 The gem should be free of cracks or inclusions.

Rule #11 The flask temperature should be between 1400° F and 1600° F during casting. You should use standard procedure for melting the metal; don't overheat the metal.

Rule #12 After casting put the flask back into the hot kiln. When the flask is in place turn the kiln off to cool.

Rule #13 Don't remove the investment from the flask until you can hold the flask in your bare hand without making funny faces.

Rule #14 Do not quench in water. Even at this point thermal shock could cause cracking in most stones.

8

GEM STONE CASTABILITY

The term precious gem stone usually refers to diamonds, emeralds, sapphires, and topaz with all others as semiprecious. Preciousness is in the eye of the beholder, in the pocketbook of the buyer, and controlled by the supply available.

List is arranged by color.

Key to the symbols:

'C' is a cabachon cut,

'F' is a faceted cut,

'O' is opaque,

'T' is transparent,

'TL' is translucent

number is hardness,

'S' means solderable

   (to solder on any stone is to take a risk)

'CC' means can cast

'CCC' means castable with a color change

'SD' means stone destroyed

'X' means not yet tested.

All italicized stones can be cast.

Color	Mineral	Hardness	Characteristics
Black	Agate (C) wide color range	6½–7	O; TL; CCC
	Hematite (C, F)	6½	O; S; CC
	Obsidian (C, F)	5	O; CCC
	Onyx (C)	6½–7	O; TL; S; CCC
Purple	Amethyst (F, C)	7	T; TL; CCC
Blue	Aquamarine (F, C)	7½	T; CCC
	Azurite (C)	4–6	O; X
	Labradorite (C)	6–7	O; X
	Lapis Lazuli (C)	5–6	O; S
	Sapphire (F, C)	9	T; TL; S; CC
	Star sapphire (C)	9	TL; S; CC
	Sodalite (C)	6	O; X
	Turquoise (C)	5–6	O; SD
Green	Agate (moss agate) (C)	7	O; TL; CCC
	Alexandrite (in daylight XF)	8½	T; X
	Amazonite (C)	6	O; X
	Aventurine (C)	7	O; X
	Bloodstone (C)	4–5	O; TL
	Chrysocolla (C)	4–5	O; TL
	Chrysoprase (C)	6½–7	T; TL
	Emerald (F)	8	T; CCC
	Nephrite Jade (C) (also white, gray, brown, black, lavender, orange)	6½–7	O; CC
	Jadeite Jade (C) (also white, gray, brown, black, lavender, orange)	6½–7	O; CCC
	Malachite (C)	4–5	O; X
	Olivine (F)	6½	T; CC
	Peridot (F)	6½–7	T; CC
	Tourmaline (F, C) (blue, green, olive, white)	7–7½	T; X
	Turquoise (C)	5–6	O; SD
Yellow	Agate (C)	7	O; TL; CCC
	Topaz (corundum or precious XF)	8–9	T; CCC
	Topaz quartz (F, C)	7	T; CCC

All synthetics have a hardness of 8 or 9. They are found in a complete color range approximating most gem stones, faceted or cabachon. They can be cast.

Some stones are dyed to enhance color.

Some stones are heat treated to obtain color.

The stones that change color (CCC) should not be discounted.

Color	Mineral	Hardness	Characteristics
Red	Agate (C)	6½–7	O; TL; CCC
	Alexandrite (incandescent light)	8½	T; X
	Carnelian (C)	7	TL; CCC
	Coral (beads or branches)	3½	O; SD
	Garnet (F, C)	6½–7½	T; C; CCC
	Jasper (C)	7	O; CC
	Ruby (F)	9	T; S; CC
	Star ruby (C)	9	TL; S; CC
	Spinel (also pink, blue, green) (F, C)	8	T; S; CC
Pink	Rodochrosite (C)	6½	O; X
	Rhodonite (C)	6½	O; X
	Rose quartz (C)	7	O; TL; CCC
	Tourmaline (F, C)	7–7½	T; CCC
Brown	Agate (C)	7	O; TL; CCC
	Amber (C, F)	2–2½	T; TL; SD
	Smoky quartz (F, C)	7	T; CCC
	Tiger eye (C) (also dyed red, blue, green)	7	O; CCC
	Agate (C)	7	O; TL; CCC
White	Diamond (F) (also yellow, coffee, black, rose)	10	T; S; CCC
	Moonstone (C) (also lt. blue, green, red, black, yellow)	6–6½	TL; CC
	Opal (C) (clear or white from Australia; orange from Mexico)	5–6	O; TL; SD
	Pearl (with green, pink, blue, brown and gray tints)	2½–4½	O; SD
	Quartz (rock crystal) (F, C)	7	T; C
	Spinel (F)	8	T; S; C
	Zircon (F) (also blue, red, green, orange, brown)	7½	T; S; CCC
	Labradorite (C)	6–7	O; X

Champagne topaz turns pink.

Jadeite turned white and gray; some call this color Imperial Jade.

Quartz can turn cloudy (the sodium content I have been told).

Some diamonds turn cloudy (also the sodium content I have been told).

Glass gems (some imitations are glass) lose their polish.

They melt during the casting process

Agates change color but not ugly.

Emeralds turn into cloudy aquamarines.

Pink tourmaline bleaches out.

Smoky quartz also bleaches out.

Tiger eye changes color but not ugly.

Onyx turns to gray—useable.

Aquamarine turns cloudy.

Gem Birthstones With Approved Alternates, Natural Gems	Month	Synthetic Corundum or Spinel Birthstone in Colors Listed
Garnet	January	Golden Sapphire
Amethyst	February	Amethyst
Bloodstone or Aquamarine	March	Aquamarine
Diamond	April	White Sapphire
Emerald	May	Green Spinel
Pearl or Moonstone	June	Alexandrite
Ruby	July	Ruby
Peridot, Sardonyx or Carnelian	August	Peridot
Sapphire	September	Sapphire
Opal or Tourmaline	October	Rose Zircon
Topaz	November	Golden Sapphire
Turquoise or Lapis Lazuli	December	Blue Zircon

9

SPRUEING

SPRUEING THE MODEL

Sprueing the wax model is the most complex process in casting.

When you think about sprueing, think about metal flowing.

To understand the properties of metal is to

understand a basic universal property of matter.

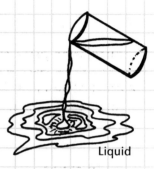
Liquid

All matter can be solid/frozen.

All matter can be liquid.

All matter can be vapor/gas.

It's just a matter of degree.

It's just matter's reaction to temperature.

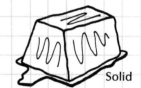
Solid

EXAMPLE: Look at water.

At one temperature group it is a liquid.

At another temperature group it is frozen solid--ice.

At another temperature group it is steam, a gas.

Gas

EXAMPLE: Look at mercury.

At one temperature group it is a liquid.

At another temperature group it is frozen to a solid.

At another temperature group, it becomes a gas and evaporates.

EXAMPLE: Look at glass.

   At one temperature group it is frozen solid.

   At one temperature group it is liquid.

   At one temperature group, it vaporizes and becomes a gas.

EXAMPLE: Look at wax.

   At one temperature group it is frozen solid.

   At one temperature group it is liquid.

   At one temperature group it becomes vapor, then gas.

EXAMPLE: Look at silver.

   At one temperature group it is frozen solid.

   At one temperatue group it is a liquid.

   At one temperature group it evaporates and becomes a gas.

In casting, you are using the properties of

   metal to your advantage.

You control metal in its frozen state,

   with sawing, filing, sanding, and buffing.

When you solder, you cause metal to become liquid and

   join two frozen pieces of metal together.

   You are controlling its frozen/liquid state.

When you fuse metal you cause metal to become liquid.

   You control the liquidness of the metal.

   You control metal in its liquid state with a mold.

   You control the flow of metal to/in the mold

   through tunnels/the melted out sprue caves.

So sprues, the solid tunnels, are most important.

More facts to understand the process.

When metal freezes, it shrinks.

When dealing with a thick/thin form,

the thin part freezes first

and in its shrinking

it will draw metal from the thick part.

When the thick part freezes, it shrinks too.

If it cannot draw metal from somewhere

to fill itself, cavities are formed.

We call these cavities pits or porosity.

Each artist that deals with this problem

develops a different answer

according to their style of wax work.

Each wax model is different because it is the

artist that makes them different.

Here are seven general observations,

perhaps laws, that will make decisions easier.

#1 Arrange the model so it won't trap air.

#2 Sprue to the thick or,

#3 Sprue to the between of thick and thin.

Use the model as a sprue.

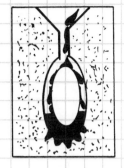

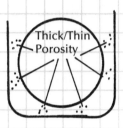

Thick/Thin Porosity

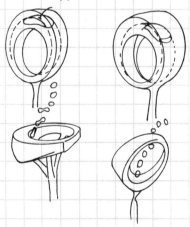

Trapped Air Bubble

No Trapped Air

#4 If your wax is 16 gauge or more,

   use sprues 10 gauge or thicker

   to get the metal up where you want it.

#5 Use thinner sprues to distribute metal.

   Sometimes, I'll use 3 gauge and

      10 gauge for the tree,

      14 gauge for the branchs,

      and about 18 gauge for very short twigs.

#6 Arrange the sprues as drains.

   If the wax will drain out

   the metal will flow in.

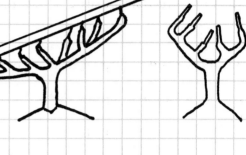

   Sprues can curve.

   They don't have to be straight.

#7 Smooth sprues where they join.

   Joints should be rounded.

Sharp joints will become

   plaster points when the wax is melted out.

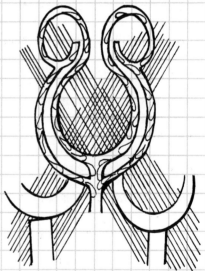

They will break when metal flows in

   and float in the metal until the metal freezes,

   causing pits in the metal.

Sprue to places where you can remove the sprue easily,

   stay away from hollows.

Sprue to places that won't change the texture.

   Narrow the sprue at or just below the contact point.

A single sprue will channel the metal best.

When sprueing rings or objects under 1½" diameter,

    such as charms, tie tacks or multiple channels,

    group the small things in one flask.

    Arranging close together is okay,

    just as long as they don't touch each other.

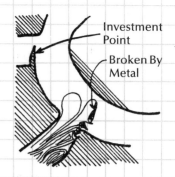

Investment Point

Broken By Metal

Most commercial houses use the tree systems for multiple casting.

Some commercial casters use the pin cushion sprueing system.

It is okay for them because they cast large amounts of metal.

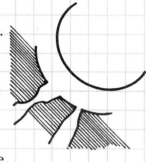

The pin cushion system is risky for the small caster.

    The small amount of metal used makes metal flow unpredictable.

    You can't be sure that all the "pins" will catch the metal.

    A single sprue leaves nothing to chance.

Don't get discouraged if things don't go as you expected.

After all, there is only experience.

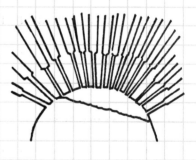

Any learning experience can be a good experience.

It's up to you to learn to use the experience.

There are degrees of learning,

    with the most learning taking place

    in an intensive problem-solving mode.

    Ask yourself, "Can I use this to solve the problem I've set for myself"?

    Reinforce your experience by telling yourself

      I like what I did.

      What I did I can use again another time.

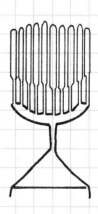

Sprue to the edge if your ring is textured,

    otherwise sprue straight in the bottom of the band.

It is a good idea to have a plain section

    on the bottom of the band.

It is a good place for a sprue and

    it also makes it easier to size if necessary.

        Cut and add metal to make the ring larger.

        Cut out metal to make the ring smaller.

Sprueing flat stuff can be tricky.

    The thinner the model the more sprues are needed.

    Use a rule of placement, the visual division method.

    Divide the piece into ¾″ squares for 12 gauge sheet wax.

    Divide the piece into ½″ squares for 20–24 gauge sheet wax.

    A single main sprue with

    branches and twigs

    channels the metal best.

Most of my students use more sprues than I do.

It isn't important how many you use, for

you can't oversprue.

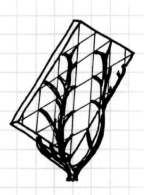

You can only undersprue.

    If the sprues do the job and the piece works,

        you used enough.

        That's all that counts.

If you undersprued, it didn't turn out.

Look and see where sprues were needed

and learn from your experience.

Use the wire joining technique described on page 58 for sprueing.

I'll usually sprue in this order.

Cover the model with twigs—20 gauge.

Add branches to top—16 gauge.

Add 12 gauge long branches.

Add a 10 gauge trunk.

Keep in mind drawing

imaginary ¾" squares on the model

with twig sprues at intersections.

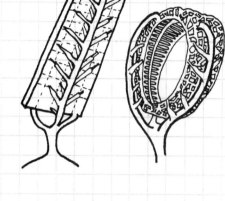

WEIGH THE MODEL

After sprueing, weigh the model.

Use the gram or dwt balance scale.

It makes no difference which measure you use.

Just use the same measure for your wax and metal.

Plastic weighs the same as wax,

except for the foam plastics.

The foam plastics use the formula of

15 times the weight of the model.

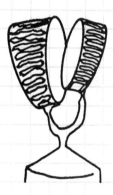

The casting weight formula for fine silver,

sterling silver, brass, nu-gold, and bronze

is 10 times the weight of the model.

The casting weight formula for gold is

   14 times the weight of the model.

   Casting weight formula for aluminum is

   5 times the weight of the model.

Actual model weight for casting is an *estimate* only!

   To estimate cost of a finished piece use the model formula of

      7 times the weight of the model for silver and brass,

      nu-gold and bronze.

      10 times the weight of the model for gold

      as the actual model weight.

The water displacement measurement is the old but good method of

model-metal measurement.

   Using a tapered cylinder,

   immerse model in water.

      The water will rise.

      Mark the water level measurement.

      Mark it plainly where you won't forget it.

      Mark the liquid starting level.

      Mark the liquid rising level.

      Put your metal in until the water rises to its mark.

10

INVESTING

MOUNTING

To mount the model for casting,

  attach the sprue to the button.

    The button forms the funnel that channels

    metal to the sprue.

The button can be part of

  the rubber flask base or

  the button can be added

  to the rubber base.

A temporary button can be made of

  wax, clay, plasticine, or

  wall cleaning putty.

The button needs to be shaped like a small mound,

which when removed makes a hole

to catch and channel the melted metal to the model.

The button can be made of a rigid material like

wood, metal or plastic.

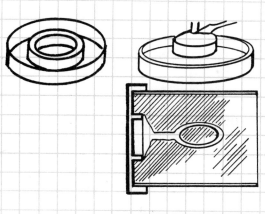

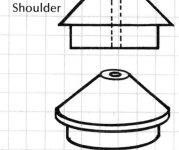

Button With Shoulder

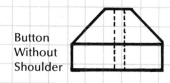

Button Without Shoulder

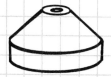

The rigid button should be smooth and

have a hole made for holding a main sprue.

Attach the sprued model to the button.

Gently put the flask in place to

check the model clearance.

The model should be at least

½" from the top of the flask.

The model should be at least

1/16" from the flask side.

Remove the flask carefully.

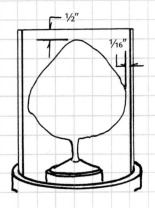

DEBUBBLIZING

To prepare the model for investing, you must debubblize.

Any time you put a solid

into a liquid

air bubbles attach.

If the bubbles are not removed,

before the investment hardens,

they form positive spheres

on the model and

become metal (with the model) when cast.

It is difficult to remove

all traces of the metal bulbs.

Debubblizer does not remove bubbles.

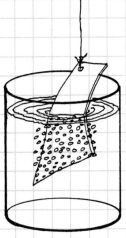

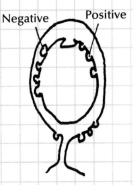

Negative   Positive

It is a surface tension-reducing agent that

makes the model slippery.

Once debubblized the bubbles will slide off easily.

There are techniques to process the investment and the model

to reduce or eliminate the bubbles.

Several ways will be covered within this chapter

on investing techniques.

Put the debubblizer on the model.

Paint it on with a brush.

Lay it on, don't stroke.

You will make bubbles

on the model by stroking too much.

Dip the model into a wide-necked jar

filled with the debubblizer liquid.

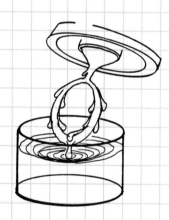

Always blow the excess liquid off the model.

There are many commercial debubblizing products.

There is not much difference between them

except for their color.

Make your own debubblizer if you wish.

Use green liquid soap or

use dish detergent.

Mix with denatured alcohol for quick drying,

1 part soap or detergent

to 3 parts alcohol.

If you can find it, add 5% aerosol liquid to the alcohol.

Don't let the debubblizer fill the holes of the texture,

unless you want them to be filled.

Blow gently so it won't puddle.

Hold your hand behind the model as you blow.

If the model breaks loose from the base,

you can catch it.

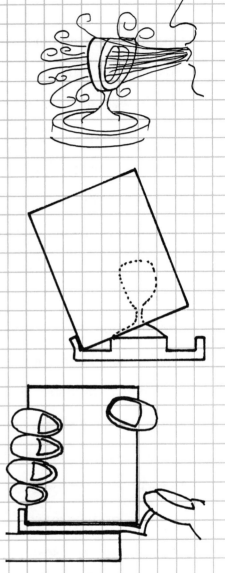

It is best to blow in short positive whoofs.

That way you won't get dizzy.

Coat the model three times.

Let the debubblizer dry between coats.

Repeat until the model turns shiny when dry.

If you are really pressed for time,

coat with debubblizer once.

Blow the model as clean as you can.

Invest the model before it becomes dry.

Sometimes flashing will occur

if too much debubblizer is

allowed to stay on the surface.

Put the flask over the mounted model—carefully.

Tilt the flask slightly to catch the edge of the rubber sprue former base.

Slide the flask and the rubber base over the edge of the table.

With your thumb and forefinger

bend the edge of the base gently.

Now rotate and ease the flask into place.

Add a paper collar to the top of the flask.

Adjust it to stick 1 ½" over the top of the flask.

Write your name, metal weight for casting

and gems (if casting in place).

Hold the collar in place with a rubber band

or a piece of tape.

Or use a commercial rubber collar.

Adjust it to be 1 ½" over the edge of the flask.

Put a scrap of paper under the bottom edge of the band.

Write your name or initials on the paper

and the metal and weight for casting.

Write "C.G.," if casting gems in place, on the paper.

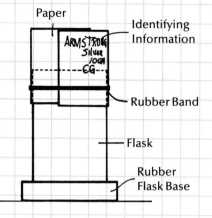

Paper

Identifying Information

Rubber Band

Flask

Rubber Flask Base

THE PROCESS OF INVESTING

Investment is a sophisticated plaster.

Its composition enables it to maintain its integrity to stress.

Investment has excellent thermal stability.

Each investment manufacturer

has its own water to investment ratio

that develops their investment to top performance.

PreVest Company of Cleveland, Ohio

uses a 38 water to 100 investment powder ratio.

On the basis of that ratio,

1 gram of water equals 2.63 grams of investment powder.

See the next page for a practical table for the mixing of *PreVest* investment.

Projected Table
(PreVest *Investment—38 Water to 100 Investment Powder Ratio*)

Flask Size	Water (gm or cc)	Investment Powder (gm)	(oz)	(lb)
2″ × 2½″	68	178.84	6.31	.39
2″ × 3″	85	223.55	7.89	.49
2″ × 3½″	102	268.26	9.46	.59
2″ × 4″	114	299.82	10.58	.66
2½″ × 3″	136	357.68	12.62	.78
2½″ × 3½″	160	420.80	14.84	.92
2½″ × 4″	182	478.66	16.88	1.05
3″ × 3″	205	539.15	19.02	1.19
3″ × 4″	274	720.62	25.42	1.59
3″ × 5″	340	894.20	31.54	1.97
3″ × 6″	410	1,078.30	38.04	2.38
3″ × 7″	500	1,315.00	46.38	2.89
3½″ × 4″	364	957.32	33.77	2.11
3½″ × 5″	456	1,199.28	42.30	2.64
3½″ × 6″	548	1,441.24	50.83	3.18
3½″ × 7″	640	1,683.20	59.37	3.711
4″ × 4″	410	1,078.30	38.04	2.38
4″ × 5″	546	1,435.98	50.65	3.17
4″ × 6″	637	1,496.95	52.80	3.3
4″ × 7″	728	1,914.64	67.53	4.22
5″ × 5″	864	2,272.32	80.15	5.01
5″ × 6″	1,000	2,630.00	92.76	5.798
5″ × 7″	1,182	3,108.66	109.65	6.85

Each manufacturer has a preferred water ratio for its

particular kind of investment powder.

Some are 38 water to 100 investment powder.

Some are 41 water to 100 investment powder.

The following list will make your water to powder to flask size easy.

100 IP to 28 W; 1 gram W = 3.57 grams IP
100 IP to 30 W; 1 gram W = 3.33 grams IP
100 IP to 32 W; 1 gram W = 3.125 grams IP
100 IP to 34 W; 1 gram W = 2.94 grams IP
100 IP to 36 W; 1 gram W = 2.77 grams IP
100 IP to 37 W; 1 gram W = 2.70 grams IP
100 IP to 38 W; 1 gram W = 2.63 grams IP
100 IP to 39 W; 1 gram W = 2.56 grams IP
100 IP to 40 W; 1 gram W = 2.50 grams IP
100 IP to 41 W; 1 gram W = 2.44 grams IP
100 IP to 42 W; 1 gram W = 2.38 grams IP

The more powder the thicker the mixture.

A cubic centimeter weighs 1 gram.

Measure the amount of water you put in your flask

by weight (grams) or liquid measure (cubic centimeters).

Take that number times the powder ratio as expressed as grams IP.

That will give you the amount of investment needed for your flask.

Enter those figures into the chart on the next page

so you'll have them when you want them.

EXAMPLE:

For an investment with a 100 to 38 ratio,

the flask I'm going to use holds 57cc of water.

$57 \times 2.63 = 134.52$ grams of IP (investment powder).

Flask Ratio Chart
(*Investment Powder and Water*)

The investment I'm using has an investment powder to water of: _____

Flask Size	Holds This Much Water	Needs This Much Powder	So the IP Ratio is:

The measurement of investment and water is

important for consistency and

accuracy of investment mixing.

Sometimes you don't have a

scale or vessel for liquid measure.

You can mix investment by ritual

rather than by formula.

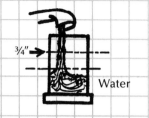

You can process the mixture this way.

After preparing your model and flask

(pick a flask that is the same size),

seal its bottom with a rubber base.

Put water in the test flask to ¾ full.

Pour the water into a mixing bowl.

Use a rubber mixing bowl,

a flexible plastic bowl or

one-half of a large rubber ball.

Sift the investment powder slowly into the water.

Use a flour sifter or

use a cupped hand

with fingers slightly spread, but

sift the powder in slowly.

Do not mix until

powder has absorbed the water and

forms cracked squares on the surface,

like dried mud.

Then mix together by hand.

Mixing by machine is not necessary.

Mixing by hand folds in less air.

The mixture should feel smooth

   and drip, not run, off your fingers.

It should be the consistency of thin pancake batter.

The formula-measured mixture is much the same.

   Put the measured water in the rubber bowl.

   Sift in the measured investment powder slowly.

   Do not mix until

   powder has absorbed the water.

   Then mix together.

Whichever method you use,

   vacuum the mixture (if you have a vacuum pump),

   until large bubbles form and break.

Air bubbles that are in the investment will attach to the model.

   They need to be shaken off or, at least,

   helped to slide off the model.

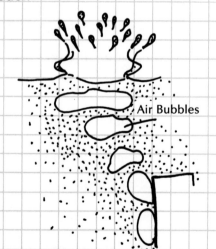

Air Bubbles

When any solid is placed into a liquid,

   air bubbles attach to the solid.

   As the air is pumped out via the vacuum machine

   the air pressure goes down.

   The air bubbles expand,

   break loose and float to the top of the mixture.

A vacuum pump and a bell jar are a great aid

but you can do without if you build a vibrating table

(see tool section, page 32)

or vibrate the filled flask by hand.

When using the vacuum machine,

make sure that the vacuum table top and

the vacuum bell jar are clean.

Some folks start by vacuuming water!

Most don't, but it can't hurt. In fact,

the least amount of bubbles in the water,

the better off you are.

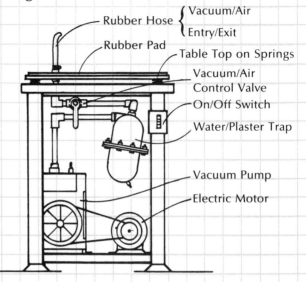

Rubber Hose { Vacuum/Air Entry/Exit
Rubber Pad
Table Top on Springs
Vacuum/Air Control Valve
On/Off Switch
Water/Plaster Trap
Vacuum Pump
Electric Motor

Mix mixture together.

Put the bowl on the vacuum table.

Cover the mixture bowl with the bell jar.

Turn on the motor.

Turn the valve to vacuum.

Listen for a change in the

sound of the motor.

Take a sponge, wet it with water and

deposit water next to the bell jar.

Wipe the joining edges of the bell jar and the table.

The deposited water will aid in sealing the bell jar.

Continue to vacuum until

large bubbles form and break.

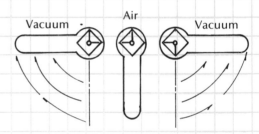

Vacuum   Air   Vacuum

Vacuum/Air Control Valve Positions

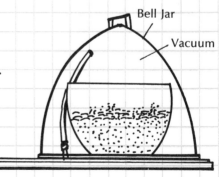

Bell Jar
Vacuum

Turn off the motor at this point.

Turn valve to let air in.

You will hear a hiss.

When the hiss stops,

lift off the bell jar.

Place it carefully on a tabletop nearby.

Pinch rubber/plastic bowl lips together

to form a pouring spout.

Pour into collared flask:

Pour to one side.

Don't hit the model.

Fill to the top of the flask.

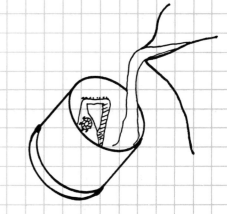

Pick up the filled flask by

the rubber sprue former.

Put it on the vacuum table.

Put on the bell jar.

Turn on the motor.

Turn the valve to evacuate air (vacuum).

Wipe the joining edges of the bell jar and the table with water.

Tap on the table to help

shake the bubbles loose.

Continue to vacuum and tap

until large bubbles form and break.

Turn off the motor.

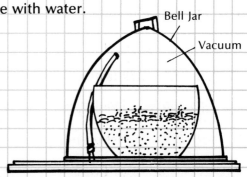

Bell Jar

Vacuum

Turn the valve to let the air in.

Lift off the bell jar.

Remove the flask holding it by

the rubber sprue bottom.

Place the flask on a shelf to harden.

It will harden in 10 to 15 minutes.

Vibrating the filled flask

can be just as effective as vacuum.

The idea is to shake the bubbles loose.

This can be as simple as

tapping on a board

that's on two bricks, with the flask on the board.

Or holding your flask

on a commercial vibrator.

Perhaps using a vibrating table

(see tool section for instructions).

Vibrate for 3 to 5 minutes or

vibrate until the investment sets.

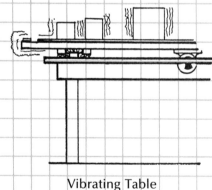

Vibrating Table

Mixed investment sets in 9 to 15 minutes.

Depending in part on your water temperature.

Warm water sets faster.

Cold water sets slower.

As soon as the investment sets,

you can start your burn out.

You can wait as long as you want

before you start burn out.

Arrange your burn out so you have time to

cast immediately.

You can let the kiln and flask

cool slowly and

cast another day, but

you run the risk of cracking the investment.

You can remove the flask from the kiln and

put it in a closed container

to cool slowly.

Cover the flask with a coffee can and

put it in a cold empty kiln, or

put it in a box of fire brick.

Use this cooling procedure

for ash removal and

for cooling the flask for casting

pewter,

tin,

aluminum and

printers lead.

11

BURN OUT

The idea of burn out is to melt out the wax model and

to vaporize the residue carbon left by the wax.

The idea of burn out is to burn or melt the plastics or

the organic material and to vaporize residue

left by the plastic or the organic material.

The idea of burn out is to clean the mold

so that its pores are clean.

The clean investment can then absorb gasses and air

as the metal rushes into the mold.

The thickness of the plastic

or the organic material will

require a longer "red soak" time.

There is such a wide variety

of plastic and organic material,

that a precise "red soak" time

is almost impossible to determine.

As a general rule, add one hour of "red soak" time

to any plastic or organic material.

"Red soak" time is the critical temperature of burn out.

That temperature is 1200° F to 1300° F.

Carbon vaporizes at 1200° F and above.

It is necessary to reach and

maintain that temperature

to clean the mold.

Your judgement of the temperature is necessary.

A pyrometer is easiest.

Its pointer tells the temperature,

but it's difficult to trust a pyrometer.

They need to be checked for

accuracy quite often.

Pyrometers

I would rather you trust your judgement and experience.

What color red is your metal

when *Handy Harmon* flux melts?

Dark cherry red—1200° F, of course.

Your eye sees its first hint

of red at 900° F.

Bright cherry red is the temperature of

easy solder when it flows

at 1350° F.

So, look in your kiln and at the flask for color.

Even take your flask out of the kiln,

tilt the sprue hole up and look at the color.

It's the sprue hole color that's important

  not the color of the metal flask.

"Red soak" is between deep red and bright cherry red.

  You can paint the flask

  with a stripe of *Handy Harmon* flux.

    The flux melts a 1200° F and gets shiny,

    a great indicator of temperature.

Air Pockets

Once you burn out in a particular kiln,

  you will be able to adjust your burn out time.

    Each kiln is different.

    Observe and learn to

    keep records to help you learn.

Make sure that your kiln is vented.

If you like to do jewelry—vent, or

you will become allergic to the fumes.

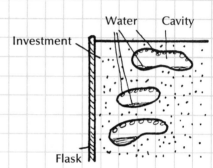

Water   Cavity

Investment

Flask

You can minimize fumes and save the wax by

  boiling your flasks in water, sprue up.

    Cover the flask with water.

    Boil the water.

    Skim up the wax.

    Take the flasks out.

    Start the burn out with wet flasks.

If you can, use a pressure autoclave

  at 10–20 psi for 20 minutes.

A pressure cooker works fine.

Put the flask in with the sprue down.

Put on a stand above the water.

Cook at 10–20 psi for 20 minutes.

Cast wet if you wish.

Burn out as usual.

Collect the wax.

A gas kiln is the best for burn out.

It gives the fastest rise in temperature,

has excellent control and

is inexpensive to run.

An electric kiln is good.

It has a steady temperature rise,

has good control and

is the safest,

most inexpensive to buy.

A wood kiln is possible.

A gas or electric hot plate can be used if vented.

Boil out the wax first.

Then use a piece of iron or steel to cover the burner.

Put the flask on a ceramic or metal stilt, the sprue down.

Cover the flask with a pyrex sauce pan or pyrex coffee pot.

Turn on low for 15 minutes for an electric hot plate and

then turn to high.

Turn on low for 15 minutes with ½" flame on a gas hot plate and

then turn the flame to spread 1" flames on the steel plate.

After 45 minutes to 1 hour, watch for the color blue of wax to appear

in investment on top of flask.

The wax will grow from a colored spot in the investment on top of the flask,

to a majority of the surface area.

In 30 minutes it will start to get

smaller and disappear.

When the wax trace is gone,

when the investment looks clean;

and the sprue hole is dull red,

it is ready to cast.

The rationale for the heat stages used during burn out.

The low setting is to heat the kiln and

warm the investment.

The medium setting is to heat the investment

to the point of removing water and wax.

The high setting is to get to the red soak temperature,

which will remove carbon residue.

The "red soak" will assure clean pores in investment,

to allow casting gases to be absorbed by the investment.

Turning the heat to low, to lower the temperature is

to permit metal to flow through the cavities in the investment

minimizing the gas developed during the investment and metal interaction.

It also allows the temperature to fall slowly to that

point where the particular metal,

theoretically, casts best.

As flask temperature drops under 800° F,

the likelihood of the mold cracking

increases.

This is due to the normal stress in investment

caused by cooling contraction of

investment and steel flask.

This tendency becomes extreme

below 600° F.

The slower the temperature drop

the safer the investment is.

All burn out procedures are variable.

They depend upon how you prepare the model and the flask.

They vary if you dry out your flask thoroughly

beforehand, or if you don't.

They vary if you get to "red soak" quickly.

They vary if you remove your wax prior to burn out.

They vary if you get to "red soak" slowly.

They vary if you are casting gem stones in place.

Then you want the flask to be hotter than normal

to minimize thermal shock, around 1400° F.

They vary with your method of debubblizing.

The casting procedures are all links in the chain for successful casting.

You need to keep a record of your casting

to realize and develop your strongest chain of events.

Exploding investment is a phenomenon that occasionally occurs.

Sometimes a flask will "blow its top" and

a "too fast" burn out is blamed.

What happens, I think, is that

water collects in large

air bubbles in the investment.

When the investment is hot enough

to turn that collected water into steam,

the steam can't pass through

the investment fast enough

to relieve pressure and

boom!

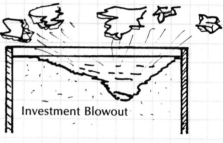

Investment Blowout

Investment is blow out of the flask.

As long as the model/cave is not

broken into, try to cast it.

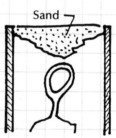

Sand

You can fill the cavity with

casting sand

to help protect from metal breakthrough,

and the metal splattering

if the metal does break through.

So remove the bubbles with vacuum or vibration.

One possible aid is to keep the moisture content in the investment even.

Some craftspersons soak the

invested flask for 1 hour

before casting.

This will insure that the investment is

the same wetness all the way through.

More about differences in burn out.

The more flasks packed into a kiln

the slower the kiln temperature will rise.

This happens because more heat has to be absorbed.

With a tightly packed kiln, all kiln setting times

should be longer in getting up to "red soak."

The red soak time can be normal.

The larger the flask diameter or

the taller the flask,

the longer the "red soak" temperature should be.

Investment is a great insulator.

The larger and/or taller flasks

take longer for the heat to penetrate

to the center of the investment.

The taller the flask and

the larger the diameter of the flask,

the slower the kiln temperature should rise.

The greater volume takes longer to dry out.

This makes for more areas of trapped bubbles.

More investment volume means more expansion stress.

Set all flasks off of kiln shelf at least ½".

This will let the air and gas circulate.

It will aid heat penetration and

help the flask relieve itself of wax.

Use metal stilts as lifts,

use cut pieces of fire brick or

use ceramic stilts.

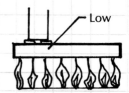

General rules of flame adjustment for gas kilns are:

Low   —the flame is just touching the shelf.

Medium—the flame is 1" over the shelf and

   the flame is spread on the bottom of the shelf 1" to 1½".

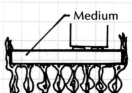

High   —the flame is 3" to 4" over the kiln shelf and

   the flame is spread on the bottom of the shelf for 2" to 3".

I know of one goldsmith

that follows the following extreme schedule.

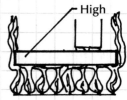

I tried it. We even worked side by side,

with my copying everything he did.

It wouldn't work for me.

My flasks would blow their tops.

His were okay—this really works for him.

Preheat electric kiln to 1300° F and put the wet flask into the kiln.

Burn out time 1 hr.

When the sprue hole glows red and the investment is clean and white take it out and cast.

Stainless steel flasks can take

higher temperatures.

Other common flask materials, such as tin cans,

cannot take the temperature over 1000° F without deterioration.

I had an electric kiln that fired with this schedule:

15 minutes on low to warm up the elements.

15 minutes on medium to warm up the elements.

Put the 3 to 10 medium-sized flasks in and

turn on high.

6 hours later the flasks would read red.

Turn to medium (to maintain the heat) for

1½ hours at red—1200° F to 1300° F.

Then turn to low to maintain 600° F to 900° F temperature for casting.

My gas kiln used this burn out schedule.

Low preheat—15 minutes.

Put four 2½" diameter by 6" flasks in the kiln.

Medium for 30 minutes.

High for 30 minutes.

Medium for 30 minutes.

Cast.

The times are always APPROXIMATE: Not hard fact.

Each kiln will fire differently.

A pyrometer is good for telling the temperature.

Just read the pointer.

Use a ceramic cone pack of

Orton standard pyrometric cones

to calibrate the pyrometer once a month.

There are two sizes of cones.

large cones	small cones
020—1175° F	020—1231° F
019—1261° F	019—1333° F
018—1323° F	018—1386° F
017—1377° F	017—1443° F
016—1458° F	016—1517° F
015—1479° F	015—1549° F
014—1540° F	

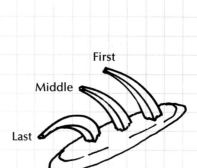

Cones Melt At Temperature

Pick three cones for the cone pack.

The middle cone is the temperature you want.

The first cone is below the temperature you want.

The last cone is above the temperature you want.

Place the cone pack where you can see it through the peep hole.

You can trust your eye to gauge

approximate temperature.

Handy Harmon flux melts at 1200° F.

Paint a stripe of *H. H.* flux on a flask.

Put that flask where you can see the stripe through the peep hole.

The first visible red the eye can see is around 900° F.

Easy solder melts at 1280° F and flows at 1325° F

which is a good cherry red.

You have the visual experience, use it.

When I use the small gas kiln at the college shop,

I follow this schedule.

For one or two flasks

2½" diameter by 3" or 4" high.

Low for 15 minutes to reach 300° F.

High for 1½ hours to 1275° F

plus or minus 50° F.

Medium for "red soak," 30 minutes.

Cast.

The burn out schedule for gas or electric kilns that

is recommended by most manufacturers

for a kiln 18" × 18" × 18" is

1 hour on low.

1 hour on medium.

4 hours on high.

3 hours on medium "red soak."

1 hour on low.

Cast.

Each metal has a prime flask temperature casting range.

Prime flask temperature for:

Yellow gold—900° F.

White gold—1000° F.

Fine or sterling silver—800° F.

Brass, bronze, nu-gold—800° F.

Aluminum—300° F.

Pewter, tin—200° F.

Printers lead—200° F.

The electric kiln schedule I use now.

Put in flasks:

15 minutes on low to warm the elements.

Turn on high.

Check flask color each hour.

Approximately 2 to 4 hours later,

turn down to medium for

1 hour of "red soak."

½ hour on low.

Keep on low while casting.

I use the gas kiln whenever I can.

It is so much faster.

But my electric holds more flasks.

12

THE CASTING PROCESS

CASTING PREPARATION BROKEN ARM MACHINE

Balancing

To balance the broken arm machine,

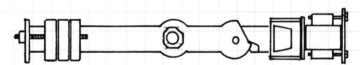

    loosen the center nut.

    Put the invested flask on the saddle.

    Keep the arms straight.

    Now turn the weights to adjust the balance.

    Approximate balance is all you can expect.

    Tighten center nut.

If you use the same size flask for casting,

    you can balance the machine

    before burn out.

You can also make the adjustment for different flasks,

    without difficulty,

    before each casting.

Winding

The broken arm machine is driven by a spring in the base.

Turn/Push the machine clockwise to feel the resistance.

Move your hands out of the way as you

let go of the machine.

The machine arm will spin suddenly and

as it spins you hear a tic ... tic ... tic ... tic.

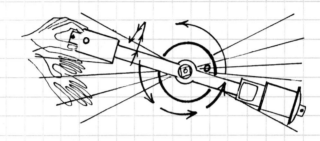

Reason For the Tic Tic

The shaft at one point in the base

is square.

There are ball bearings in an angled cave that opens to the

square part of the shaft.

Counterclockwise the square of the shaft

pushes the bearings out of the way—tic ... tic ... tic.

Turn the arm clockwise and

the square traps the ball

and locks it to the spring.

The result is resistance and the winding action starts.

Open Tic Tic

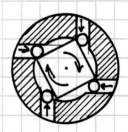

Jammed and Ready
to Wind Up

You can wind the arm with or

without a flask in place.

Wind the arm clockwise 1½ to 2 turns.

Pull/place the holding pin in front of the arm.

Use just enough pin to rest the arm against it.

This is important: Position the other part of the arm

to its right angle casting position.

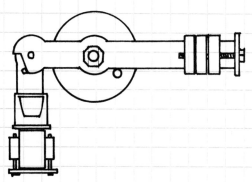

Checking the Crucible.

After you position the arm,

before you slide the fluxed crucible in place,

make sure that the crucible's hole is open.

Make sure that it

lines up with the crucible back plate hole.

Move the crucible carriage toward the nut.

This will give you room for flask placement.

Move the flask saddle so

the flask will balance on it.

The crucible is a refractory ceramic.

It is made to stand the stress of

extreme changes of temperature.

To flux the crucible

heat it with a torch to red.

Put in a four finger pinch of flux.

Any casting flux or borax will do.

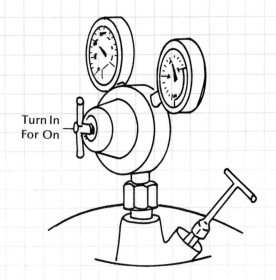

Turn In
For On

Lighting The Acetylene Torch

Gauge Shows the
Pressure of the
Gas in the Tank

Gauge Shows the
Pressure of the
Gas in the Hose

Lighting the Acetylene Torch

First, the gauges (there are two).

This one, the one with big numbers tells you how much gas is in the tank. If it reads "zero" turn the long rusty handle clockwise. If it reads another number it's ready to go (if not the tank is empty).

The gauge with lower numbers shows the pressure of the gas on the hose to the torch. To adjust that pressure, turn the handle that's between the gauges so it moves in.

As you turn the handle the needle in the gauge will start to move.
Keep turning the handle until the needle points between 8 and 10.

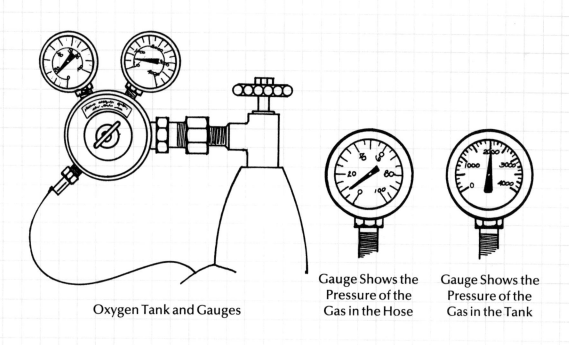

Oxygen Tank and Gauges

Gauge Shows the
Pressure of the
Gas in the Hose

Gauge Shows the
Pressure of the
Gas in the Tank

Turning on Oxygen and Natural Gas

First the natural gas.

If the handle is in line with the gas pipe, the gas is on.

Now the oxygen gauge and tank.

The gauge with the big numbers up to 2000 tell you how much oxygen is in the tank in pounds (2,000 means 2,000 pounds of oxygen is in the tank). If it reads "zero," turn the handle on top of the tank counterclockwise. The gauge should register more than 25 when turned on. Less than 25 is not enough pressure to cast with. The gauge reads pounds of oxygen pressure.

The gauge with the smaller numbers up to 50 pounds tells you the oxygen pressure on the line and to the torch. Turn the "T" handle clockwise to allow oxygen to flow to the torch.

Watch the gauge while turning the handle slowly
Keep turning until the needle points to 8 pounds pressure.

Heat the inside of the crucible with the torch.

When the flux melts, pick up the crucible with tongs.

Tilt the crucible to run the flux around on the inside.

Crucibles come in several ounce-capacity sizes,

from 1 oz, 2½ oz, 7 oz, 12 oz and 20 oz of gold.

Use the size recommended for your machine.

The fluxing of the crucible

bonds and seals the inner surface.

It prevents the metal from

melting into the crucible.

It provides a smooth surface

so the metal will release easily when it is heated.

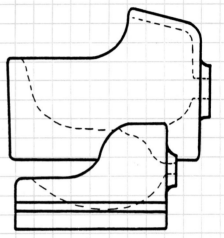

2½ oz
5 oz
7 oz
9 oz
12 oz
20 oz
25 oz

Use a different crucible for each kind of metal.

It is best to use clean metal.

Pickle, bright dip or sand blast the metal.

Be careful to use a minimum of flux

on the metal when casting.

Crucible should last a long time.

Flux can build up on a crucible and plug the exit.

To clean a crucible:

You can heat the crucible to melt the flux and then scrape it off.

You can also heat to melt the flux

when in the casting machine.

Wind the machine 3 or 4 times.

With the empty flask in place,

heat crucible to melt the flux and release.

Do this several times.

CASTING PREPARATION STRAIGHT ARM MACHINE

The straight arm machine is

used primarily with large flasks.

6″ maximum diameter to 3″ minimum diameter.

8″ maximum length to 3″ minimum length.

The usual size of the flask used with this machine is 4″ by 6″.

The crucible capacity available is 12 oz of gold and 20 oz of gold.

Maximum for silver, brass or bronze would be 2 oz less.

Balancing

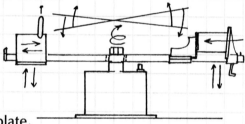

To balance, you first need to

loosen the center nut.

Hold the flask centered against the ringed back plate.

Slide the flask and back plate forward

to wedge the flask against the crucible baffle.

Tighten the back plate in place.

Lift the weight pin and

slide the weight to adjust the balance.

Add more weight rings if it is necessary.

Then tighten the center nut to secure the arm.

Winding

The winding mechanism is spring driven.

It operates much like the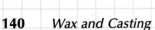

broken arm machine.

Wind it up clockwise 2 to 3 turns.

The flask is so large and heavy

that the arm needs assistance at the start of the release.

Just a flip-of-the-wrist type push.

Checking the Crucibles

The large crucibles can hold up to 20 oz of gold.

Pretreat the crucible with the same fluxing technique

used on the littler crucibles.

Add as many pinches of flux as necessary

to cover the inside of the crucible

where metal contact might be made.

It is safer to put the flask in place,

and then wind the machine

and lean it against the holding pin so it

won't release before it is ready.

Before casting, make sure the vent over the casting area is turned on,

the flask is in place,

the machine is wound and the arm

is leaning against its holding pin.

CASTING

Light the torch and

    adjust the flame for its covering power and efficiency.

    Put one-quarter of your metal in the crucible.

        The metal should be clean, cut in small pieces and

        none should stick over the edge of the crucible.

Angle the torch so that the flame circles

    the crucible interior

    without cutting across itself.

        Cutting across itself can cause the flame to blow out

        or sputter.

When the metal is hot, add a pinch of flux.

    Continue to heat while the metal draws to itself.

Add another quarter of the metal.

Repeat until all of your metal draws to itself.

Old metal might need a small two-finger pinch of flux for each addition of metal.

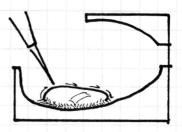

Heat until the flux cleans the top of the melted

    metal until it is shining like a mirror.

    Sometimes a crust will form on the top

    of the molten metal.

    The crust can prevent the melting of the metal.

    It can easily be removed.

    When the crust forms

    pull your torch away, just for the count of three.

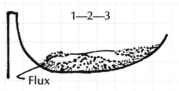

1—2—3

Flux

Put the torch back on the metal.

Do it several times if necessary.

Usually the crust will break up

within two tries and be pulled

to the crucible walls.

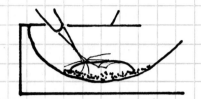

The melted metal's surface will be mirror-like.

A thin steel rod is handy for cleaning

large impurities from the top of the molten metal.

Heat the rod to orange-red heat and the metal will not stick

to the rod, just impurities will be collected.

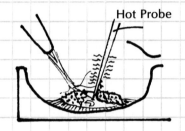

Hot Probe

As soon as the metal is clean

and is thoroughly melted,

prepare to release the casting arm.

Remember to count to three out loud

  so people near you won't be startled by the release.

Hold the torch handle horizontally to the machine.

Keep the flame on the metal to the last microsecond.

Reach out and pull the casting arm so the holding pin drops.

Release on the count of three.

Take care to remove the torch and self

  from the path of the spinning arm.

Always use a gentle motion, like a dance.

  Release the arm, lift torch and hands and step back.

Alternate casting techniques for the straight arm machine

A torch sometimes has problems with masses of metal

over 3 ounces, 90 grams.

An alternate system of melting the metal is

a crucible furnace.

The crucible furnace comes in two basic types,

gas and electric.

The electric furnace is portable and

works very well.

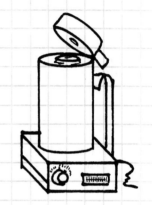

It comes in several sizes going from

30 oz of gold to 100 oz of gold.

The total weight of the unit does

make it awkward to use.

The furnace uses a replaceable graphite crucible.

The gas crucible furnace

is a stationary furnace that

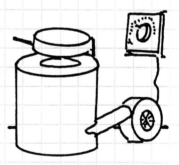

comes in many sizes, going from

100 oz of gold to 25 lbs of gold.

It also uses graphite crucibles.

The furnace can be best used

for melts of over 3 ounces.

Smaller melts cool too rapidly for

this technique.

A casting procedure with the gas crucible furnace.

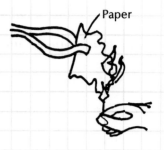

Paper

For this dialog it is assumed that the

straight arm has been balanced and

that the burn out is in the

last stages of cool down for casting.

Remember to turn on the vent.

To light the furnace, open the lid.

Twist a half sheet of paper towel.

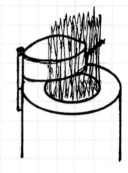

Light the paper and drop it into the furnace

in front of the gas port.

Turn on the air, set at its lowest setting.

Turn on gas.

The furnace will light with a poof!

Turn the dial to add the air until you hear a steady throb sound.

Treat the furnace as you would any gas/air torch.

Let the furnace run empty for 15 minutes.

The inside of the furnace must be glowing red

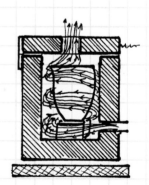

to develop continuous gas burning

when the crucible is put into the furnace.

Put the metal into the crucible and

don't let any stick out.

Put the crucible in furnace, using tongs and center it as best you can.

Close the lid.

Adjust the gas and the air.

Remember that this is just an oversized gas and air torch.

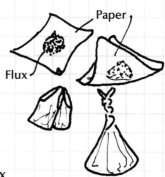

Paper

Flux

Adjust the gas and the air to an efficient flame.

In 15 minutes,

when the metal is red,

add a flux bomb.

Make the bomb by adding a four-finger pinch of flux or borax

to a square of paper towel.

Fold up and twist closed.

Drop the bomb through the hole in the lid.

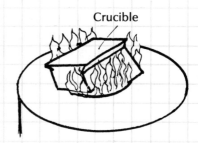

Crucible

Put the casting machine crucible

over the furnace lid vent hole.

Preheat the crucible to a bright red glow.

Remove every 15 minutes

to check on degree of melt.

When the melt is assured

and the casting crucible is glowing very red, it is the time to cast.

Put the model flask into the machine.

Wind the arm of the casting machine

and set the holding pin.

POURING THE METAL

During the pouring of the metal,

wear all of your protective clothing.

This sequence

needs to be practiced with two people.

The action needs to be smooth,

without hesitation.

Practice with cold objects.

Practice will pay off in successful castings.

One person takes the very hot casting crucible with tongs and

   slides it onto the casting carriage.

The second person pulls the casting arm and holds it.

   The holding pin drops out of the way.

   The arm is ready for release.

Take the crucible from the furnace.

Pour the molten metal into the crucible,

using a steady stream rather than a large gulp of metal.

As soon as all of the metal is poured,

the person pouring says "GO."

Person number two releases the arm with a helping push.

If you don't move rapidly and smoothly

   the casting crucible will cool and

   about one-half of your metal will freeze

   in the crucible.

   You will end up with an incomplete cast.

So practice the sequence

   and be confident of your actions.

If anything interrupts the sequence, start over.

The most important item is the red heat of the casting crucible.

SAFETY

Casting safety is important.

Make sure that you have a metal shield around your machine.

Molten metal can break through and spray during casting.

The investment can be cracked before casting.

The model was too close to the top or side of the mold.

The flask was not filled up to the top with investment.

The metal was beyond the capacity of the crucible.

The crucible gate hole was plugged.

The broken arm casting machine's free arm was not in a closed position.

Wear protective clothing for casting.

Use a leather apron, leather or asbestos gloves,

and goggles or face shield.

When the machine slows enough to stop easily, do so.

Remove the flask from the machine.

If casting stones in place, set the flask in a kiln or cover up.

In the regular casting procedure for after casting,

set the flask aside sprue up.

When the metal button is no longer red,

shield it from light when looking,

it is ready for investment removal.

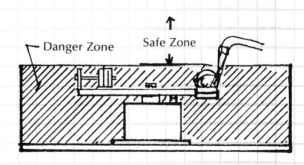

Danger Zone   Safe Zone

13

INVESTMENT
AND SPRUE REMOVAL

You can remove the investment as soon as the cast button turns dark.

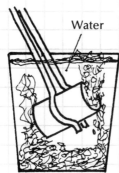

Water

Pick up the flask with tongs

and slosh it in water.

Sloshing up and down will help remove the investment.

The water and investment will rumble, hiss and sputter.

When the hissing and sputtering stops,

put the flask aside and fish out the cast metal.

Then clean the remaining investment from the flask.

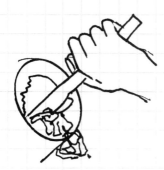

Put the cleaned flask onto the rack.

Hang up the tongs.

Investment removal with stones is different.

The first rule is to let the flask cool slowly.

When the flask is room temperature,

put the flask sideways on a table.

Tap the flask gently with a hammer,

while rolling the flask.

When investment breaks into chunks,

push the chunks into a waste basket.

Don't hit the flask near its edge,

the flask will distort.

As soon as cast, the object is visible,

keep the investment chunks

until the success of the casting is assured.

If the stone is not in set,

pulverize the investment chunks.

Carefully sift through them.

Stones can fall out of the set

during investing.

Check the investment around

the sprue former at the seat of the flask.

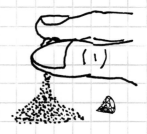

Complete investment removal from your casting is necessary.

If you've cast a stone,

use a pick first, and

a toothbrush second.

A high pressure water jet is very effective.

Don't use a sand blaster unless you've covered the stone.

To protect a gem stone from the blast of glass beads

use rubber cement or

masking tape.

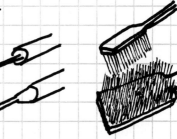

Cleaning a normal casting,

use a pick, then a brush.

Use the sand or glass blaster.

Remove all investment before cutting off the sprues.

It is important to see what to cut.

It is important to see where to cut.

Sprue removal is important as it sets the stage

for the start of the finishing process.

Clip sprues with a side cut nipper or

an end cut nipper

on light weight sprues 18 gauge and less.

A compound action

side cut nipper or

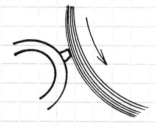

end cut nipper can be used

on medium and heavy sprues 10 gauge and less.

A jewelers saw should be used

on heavy and heaviest sprues 6 gauge and less.

Once sprues are removed,

remove all traces of the

remaining sprue joinings that you can.

Use a flexible shaft with

abrasive disks,

small carborundum or

bright boy wheels, and

bright boy bullets.

Use jewelry files in a variety of file shapes as the surface requires.

Use engravers to clean up those hard to get at corners.

14

THE FINISHING
OF CAST JEWELRY

Some pieces shouldn't be put to the polishing wheel.

They should be rubbed with steel wool or pumice,

sand or glass blasted.

Sometimes a soft finish is the best finish.

Pumice is a natural mineral of volcanic origin.

It comes in coarse or fine grain.

You can make a paste of it and

rub it on the metal

with cloth, fingers or

a toothbrush.

The technique gives a soft matte finish.

Good idea to mask the areas you don't wish to abrade.

Use a mask to protect linked surfaces,

painted surfaces or

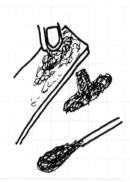

on oxidized surfaces.

Steel wool is fine strands of steel, balled into a pad form.

It comes in coarse, medium, fine and extra fine grades.

Steel wool actually scratches the surface.

Use the pattern that the scratches make.

Stroke in one direction,

or bunch the steel wool and twist for swirls.

Use the technique on polished surfaces.

Use also on markered, painted or oxidized surfaces.

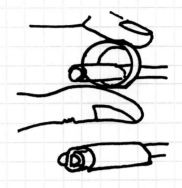

Finishing the inside of rings.

The inside is the most important

part of the finishing of a ring.

If the inside is near perfect and highly polished

the outside can be anything.

People will recognize that the outside was deliberate

and not a lack of knowledge or skill.

The same philosophy applies to pins, pendants, bracelets and

all jewelry; perhaps all art.

If the parts not on view are finished with deliberate excellence,

the parts that are on view will be recognized

as deliberate artist choices.

The inside of rings then, are most important.

The finishing starts with the wax.

Work your wax to perfection.

Sand and polish the inside of the band with

400 grit wet or dry cloth.

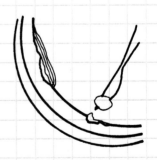

Wrap the abrasive cloth around a mandrel or

a ¼ dowel rod.

Stroke the inside to see the low spots.

Fill the hollows with wax.

Stroke, sand and smooth again.

Polish the inside with paper

on a mandrel or a dowel rod.

After casting, cleaning, and the sprues are removed.

400 grit wet or dry cloth

is used on the metal.

Cut into 3″ × 3″ squares.

Wrap it on a mandrel,

wrap it on a ¼″ dowel or

wrap it on a buffing spindle.

Secure it with tape on the mandrel and dowel.

A metal wire,

wood washer,

steel washer with inside filed sharp or

a rigid plastic washer

can hold the cloth to the buffing spindle.

If rough, use 220 grit.

Then use 320 grit.

End with 400 grit.

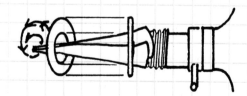

A file is still the most effective method.

  Use a #2 cut, half round ring file first.

  Then use a #4 cut, half round ring file.

    Don't drag the file or

    you'll make deep scratches.

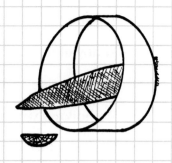

The important thing about the ring band

  is that it MUST FIT.

  When finishing, you must check the size often.

  You must know when to quit sanding

    and polish the hollows.

Polishing hollows is not difficult.

  Use rubberized abrasive

    in bullet shapes that come in

    coarse, medium and fine grades.

    They fit on flexible shaft mandrels.

  You can also use cotton *Q-Tips,*

    small felt cones or, my favorite,

    a wooden match without the head.

  Use the wooden match

    with any of the compounds.

    Use them in a drill press or

    flexible shaft.

Go to the buff for the final touch, using tripoli and/or rouge.

For the inside of ring bands use the felt ring sticks that

    fit on a tapered spindle.

For general hard-to-get-at places, use the felt bullet shaped cones that

    fit on a tapered spindle.

After buffing, clean with a mixture of detergent and water, using a soft brush.

File and sand those edges that would

    make the wearer uncomfortable.

    Don't remove much, just enough so

    the edge is not sharp.

Polish the edges smooth and clean.

Stamp your hallmark on the band.

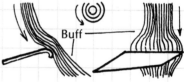

Stamp the metal symbol on the band.

Now, work on the rest of the ring.

FINISHING THE CASTING

Buffing

The buffer is just an electric motor and a tapered spindle

    that has a screw-type thread to hold the buffs in place.

At a low speed, 1,725 rpm, the buff is soft and spreads.

The Buff Is Soft and Spreads

At a high speed, 3,450 rpm, the buff is hard and tight.

The buffing units that are sold complete with a dust collector are best.

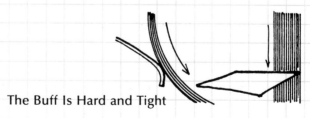

The Buff Is Hard and Tight

Some buffers have two spindles.

One has a right-hand thread.

The other is a left-hand thread.

The buffers supply the power.

The buffs provide the working surface.

The compounds do the work.

The buff for the coarse compound is made of cotton muslin.

The buff for the fine compounds is made of cotton flannel.

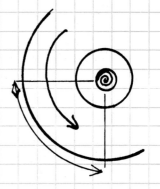

These are standard soft buffs and

are used at two speeds.

Only use the front bottom quarter of the buff.

Work from the CENTER of your piece

to the edge away from you.

Stroke the piece toward you as you

hold it firmly to the wheel.

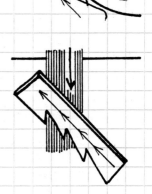

If your piece has spines or chunks,

work the buff gently with

the points away from you.

Work from the center to the points.

The wheels used for buffing and polishing.

The bristle brush wheels are very effective with texture.

The bristles flex to surface variation.

The bristles don't grab.

They come in several widths and diameters.

Hard felt wheels fill a need that

soft wheels can't fulfill.

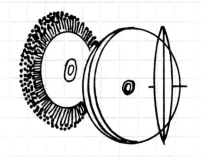

They keep the edges crisp.

They keep the edges flat as

they aid in the buffing and polishing.

The felt wheels come in many sizes and shapes.

The buffing compounds are abrasives in a grease or wax base.

There are four main compounds used in the buffing and polishing process.

Bobbing compound is very fast cutting, has a coarse grain and leaves a dull finish.

Tripoli compound is fast cutting, has a medium grain and leaves a dull finish.

White diamond compound is medium cutting, has a medium grain, and leaves a soft luster.

Red, black, or white rouge compound is slow cutting, has a fine grain and leaves a high luster.

Do not mix the compounds on the buffs or wheels.

It is most important to use a separate buff or wheel for each compound.

Wash the jewelry piece between each buffing and polishing.

Trumming is where you put compound

on a coarse string or

strip of cloth or

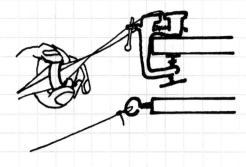

leather and, with it, stroke the metal.

Put your string in a vise.

Wrap the string around your piece and

rub it against the string as

you hold the string tight.

If your castings have pits or porosity

you might consider it an

act of God and beyond your control.

You can't fill them with solder.

Solder just won't fill holes.

You can cap them with a band of metal.

You can drill them out

and plug the hole with wire.

You might be able to peen them closed

with a hammer.

Sometimes the pits are sharp points that

get larger as you file or sand.

Chances are, that it was a piece of investment

that broke off a sprue joint and floated to the edge.

If the pitted area is spongy, it is likely that

the thick/thin draw of the metal was the problem.

Watch the wax on the next one and

learn from your experience.

In most cases it is best to finish the piece to a clean polish.

Then add a surface texture to the pitted area.

Ring Band
Section

Investment
Fragments

Rarely will you abrade the entire surface of a piece.

You can oxidize to darken an area.

You can apply color to the metal

  with acrylic paints,

  permanent inks or

  permanent magic markers.

The abraded or textured surface shows more

  with dark/light or bright/dull contrast.

Develop this contrast with oxidizers.

  Put on, wipe off.

  Put on, let dry and

  then scratch/texture with

  steel wool,

  sand paper or

  a scribe.

Oxides are chemical finishes that darken or color parts of your piece.

  The process is also called antiquing.

  The most common chemical used is liver of sulfur.

  Liver of sulfur is the common name for potassium sulfide.

  It is usually available at any pharmacy.

  It is prepared by dropping a ¼″ chunk into a pint of hot water.

  Immerse the object (copper or sterling silver) into the solution.

  When it turns blue-black, immediately remove and rinse in water.

You can also dip a swab of cotton, a brush, or steel wool swab and

brush, or rub the oxide on.

If the finish does not take in spots,

rub the spots with the washed steel wool.

Dunk the piece into the solution again.

To get the desired contrast,

buff lightly with rouge,

rub with steel wool or

rub with pumice.

For a darker finish rub with wax or light oil.

An interesting but dangerous green patina or finish for copper or bronze.

Dissolve some copper in 20% nitric acid

until the solution is saturated with copper.

Paint the solution on your piece and heat it with a torch.

Burn off the nitric, thus leaving a copper oxide on the surface.

Repeat as necessary for your green color.

But use only IN A VERY WELL-VENTILATED AREA.

Even then, avoid the fumes. Wear a proper mask.

The fumes are dangerous and can "burn" the lungs.

The Butler finish gives a frosty look to sterling silver,

that won't tarnish easily.

Heat the piece to red.

Cool the piece to black.

Drop the piece immediately into denatured alcohol.

Have a container lid handy.

If you drop metal that is too hot you'll ignite the alcohol.

Just put the lid on and

the flames will go out.

Another, more dangerous process uses acid.

Heat the piece to red.

Drop into standard buffered sulphuric acid, called pickle.

Drop into 25% nitric and water solution.

Always mix acid to water.

You must use these processes in a well vented area.

THESE FUMES ARE DANGEROUS TO YOUR HEALTH.

They can permanently damage your lungs.

The idea of a bright dip and butler finish is the same.

The acid eats the copper in the surface.

Heating the piece to red brings copper to the surface again.

Quenching while red gives the most violent action of acid.

Bright dip uses sulphuric acid in a very strong solution.

Sulphuric acid to equal amounts of water.

Mix the 50% solution in a glass container with a lid.

Heat the piece to red.

Quench in the bright dip (acid-water mix).

Heat the piece to red.

Quench in the bright dip.

Repeat the process three to ten times.

The technique builds up the parent metal.

Silver develops a pure silver skin.

Gold gets a pure gold skin.

When the pure metal is formed on the surface,

the surface becomes matte dull.

To brighten the surface,

burnish with a brass brush and soap or detergent.

Brass will burnish the surface bright.

Don't buff, for

buffing will remove the layer of pure metal.

VENT! THESE FUMES ARE DANGEROUS TO YOUR HEALTH.

WEAR PROTECTIVE CLOTHES AND FACE SHIELD.

THESE SOLUTIONS CAN BURN YOU.

Always add the acid to the water.

You start with the

weakest solution.

Add acid to make it stronger.

15

GRAVITY CASTING

Gravity casting is the oldest casting technique.

    The size of the casting determines the casting method.

        If the model doesn't fit the casting flask or

        if the flask is not going to fit into

        the casting machine,

        use the gravity pour technique.

    The weight of the casting also determines the casting method.

        If the amount of the metal needed is too much

        for your crucible, use the gravity pour.

Gravity casting uses a lower temperature of burn out.

    The gate and vent sprue system:

        Does not need to burn out as clean.

        Does not need to burn out all the carbon.

        Does not need to use stainless steel flasks for casting.

Gravity pour can use large commercial kitchen tin cans,

    well casings, or even

    5 gallon paint cans.

A model for gravity pour is made heavier.

The wall thickness should be at least 1/16".

In most products, the larger the piece,

the thicker the wall.

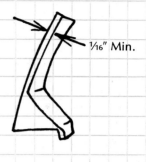

1/16" Min.

Pin all of the hollow sections to hold the "core" in place.

It is best to use a like metal for pins.

The pins must stick out beyond the wax to hold.

It is important to pin from several directions to

prevent the "core" from shifting when pushed by the incoming molten metal.

The sprue system for a gravity pour

is different and more complex than a centrifugal system.

GATE and VENT are names for sprues with specific functions.

A GATE is where metal goes in.

GATES should be thick.

Main gates should be 1/2" minimum thickness.

The larger the piece,

the thicker the gate.

A gate to the bottom of a piece

can split to several entries.

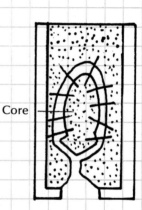

Core

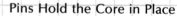

Pins Hold the Core in Place

A VENT is the sprue where the air goes out.

VENTS can be thinner than gates.

Vents normally come from the tops of the piece.

They can start small and

join together to a larger vent.

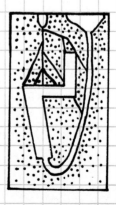

Large vents are sometimes called risers.

Make a cup at the top of the exit/end of the riser/vent.

The cup will show when the casting is full.

Thin vents will sometimes spit metal when full.

It is good to join the vents together

to make a riser/vent.

The larger the piece, the larger the vents and riser.

10 or 12 gauge wax wire is good as a vent.

Use drinking straws singly as a vent.

Use drinking straws joined as a group, as a riser.

Use 6 gauge wax wire as a riser.

Make your own risers by

rolling wax or pour them ¼" to ½" thick.

Two methods of spruing gates that come to us from history.

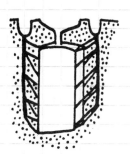

Direct pour is the earliest historical technique.

The metal goes in at the top of the model.

The air comes out of the sides and top.

It is the easiest technique to sprue up.

Direct Pour

Indirect pour was developed for large precise castings.

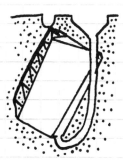

The metal goes in at the bottom of the model.

The air comes out of the top and sides of the model.

It is more difficult to set up, but I believe it is the best technique.

The incoming metal pushes air and gasses out ahead of it.

Gasses don't mix with metal, as they do with the direct method.

Indirect Pour

The tree system of sprueing for gravity pour

is good for many small objects.

It is a combination of the direct and indirect pouring methods.

The tree system uses a large main gate with

smaller leader gates.

It also uses small leader vents with

larger main risers.

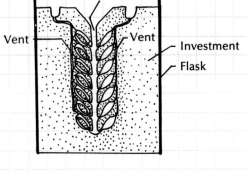

All the rules/guides of sprueing gates still apply.

Watch for areas that would cup air.

Recognize and feed to prevent the thick/thin porosity.

Sprue to places where you can easily remove the sprues.

The wax to metal ratio is the same as for centrifugal casting.

There is a difference.

In centrifugal casting,

you weigh the model without its sprue funnel/button.

So, the wax metal formula includes approximately 30% more metal

just for the button.

A great system for small castings.

$$
\begin{array}{rl}
WW \times 10 = & \text{Casting weight} \\
WW \times 7 = & \text{Estimate weight} \\
\hline
3 = & 30\% \text{ Button weight}
\end{array}
$$

In the gravity pour system you make the gates, gate funnel

and vents and vent riser as part of your piece.

All are weighed.

Weight of the wax times 7 plus "some for the pot" is correct.

It is a good idea to add some extra to allow

for air bubbles or flashing or

that occasional crucible hang back.

How much extra metal for the pot depends on the size of the casting.

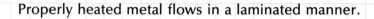
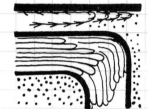
Laminate Flow

Properly heated metal flows in a laminated manner.

The metal pushes gases aside

instead of mixing with and absorbing them, thus

minimizing porosity.

Overheated metal has a lower viscosity

which encourages gas absorption.

It has a tendency to

flow in a turbulent manner.

Turbulent Flow

The turbulence encourages

the metal to mix easily with the gasses.

This is one factor that causes

porosity to form.

Make your own flask base for the larger casting containers.

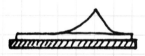
Flask Base

You can use soft wax,

clay or plasticine.

Mount the material on a square of plywood or masonite.

Spread the soft material in a larger

diameter pattern than the flask.

Shape into a smooth flat plane ⅛" thick.

Press the flask gently into the surface just to mark the material.

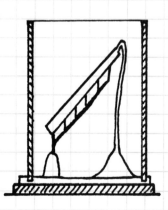

Position the sprued model.

Check the flask clearance carefully.

The model must not touch the flask.

The model must not touch the prepared base.

There must be at least 1½" clearance between the model and the casting base.

Remove the flask carefully.

Attach the gate and vent cups to the base material.

Brush on the debubblizer.

   Blow the debubblizer smooth with compressed air.

      Use 20 lb pressure and

      stay 12 inches away from the model.

Two basic methods of investing, plus variations are available for your use.

   Both techniques have been used with centrifugal casting investing.

   In technique number one, debubblize the model three times or

      until the model system is shiny.

   Put the flask in place.

   Work more material around the outside of the flask

      to seal it thoroughly 1 inch above the base.

   Mix the investment and pour to the side of the flask,

      being careful not to move the model.

   You can vibrate the flasked system on a vibrating table.

      Stay with it as it vibrates the bubbles loose,

      as leaks can develop easily.

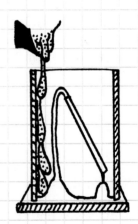

Number two technique is to apply a coat of investment to the model system

before pouring the investment to fill the flask.

Painting the model with investment can be messy.

Mix just a handful of investment at one time.

A large amount of investment will set up before you can use it all.

Lay the investment on the model with a brush.

Kind of ooze it on,

so you won't trap air bubbles.

A thin layer is all you need.

Just enough investment to cover the wax completely.

Be sure that no wax shows.

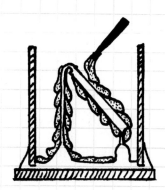

Another technique for applying investment

is to flip it onto the model system with force.

Pick up some investment with your fingers

and flip your hand at the piece.

It is messy but is the best technique for larger pieces.

Set a cardboard box on a table

with the open top facing you.

Put the model system in and flip the investment.

The flip spreads the investment thin.

Let one layer set.

The add another coat.

Cover with the flask.

Add a coil of the sealing material to the base.

Pour in the prepared investment on the side of the flask.

Don't hit the model.

Fill to top of flask.

When the investment has set, remove the completed system from the base.

Trim the cups if necessary to make the pour easier.

The advantage of the flip is that you

don't need a vacuum or vibration to minimize bubbles.

You can add one-third part crumbled old investment

to two-thirds parts of new investment mix, to save a little.

You don't need to use a debubblizing solution.

The disadvantages of the flip technique are that it is an extra step.

It is messy.

It is difficult to use on a complex wax model.

The flip can trap little air bubbles.

Suspending the model system in the flask can be difficult.

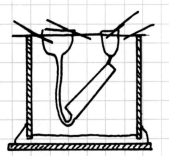

Add coat hanger wire to the outside of the gate and vent cups.

You can make tabs for hanging the model.

The wires should be long enough to span the flask.

Debubblize first, then

suspend in the flask.

Check for proper clearance at all points.

The model should be at least 1½" from the bottom.

Remove the system from the flask.

Add the investment coat.

Let the investment set on the model.

Add another coat if necessary.

Suspend in the flask.

Mix and pour the investment.

An alternate technique is to

remove the model system from the flask

after a clearance check.

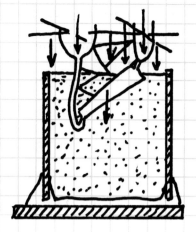

Mix the investment and

pour into the flask up to three-quarters of the flask.

Place invested wired model system down into the investment.

The investment should overflow a bit. If not,

add more investment to fill the flask to the top.

BURN OUT

Burn out is the most controversial part of the casting process,

and is the most variable.

But first, HAVE A GOOD VENT SYSTEM.

FUMES FROM BURN OUT ARE HAZARDOUS TO YOUR HEALTH.

TURN ON YOUR VENTS and keep them on until your kiln is cold.

Electric kilns are slower to heat than gas kilns.

The burn out schedule will change with the flask size.

Larger flasks need a longer burn out time.

They need a longer medium heat time until wax starts to melt,

and you can hear it snap and crackle.

They need a longer high heat time to reach the "red soak" temperature.

An electric kiln schedule. A cold kiln with a 20″ × 28″ chamber dimension, and a flask size of 8″ diameter × 18″ high.

low	1 hour	0° F to 200° F.
medium	2 hours	200° F to 500° F.
high	3 hours	500° F to 1100° F.
cherry red, medium	4 hours	1100° F to 1100° F.
barely dull red, low	1 hour	1100° F to 700° F. Ready to cast.

Another electric kiln schedule, the same kiln, the same flask.

low	1 hour	0° F to 200° F.
cherry red, high	4 hours	200° F to 1100° F.
barely dull red, low	3 hours	1100° F to 700° F. Ready to cast.

PREPARATION OF THE FLASK, TOWARD THE POURING OF THE METAL

Remove the flask from the kiln.

Place the flask in a large 36″ container,

like a galvanized laundry tub that

is one-third full of sand.

With the flask in place, add one-third more sand.

Take the crucible from the furnace and

rest it on a fire brick pad.

Position the crucible in a pouring holder.

Lift the pouring rack and crucible into a pouring position.

Tilt slowly, steadily, and

position for the flow arch of the pouring metal.

Pour slowly and steadily,

until you see metal appear

in vent/riser cups.

Stop pouring now.

Pour the extra metal into the sand bucket.

Let the poured flask cool overnight.

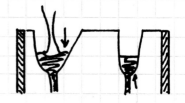

Sometimes the metal will stay molten in the flask for several hours.

Sudden cooling of a large mass of metal can cause porosity,

cracks and the crystalization of metal.

The next day, turn the flask on its side.

Tap with a hammer to break up the investment.

Clean off the investment with a wooden pick.

Sand blast the model system clean.

FINISHING THE GRAVITY POUR CASTING

There is a tendency to focus on small areas while finishing.

It is important to consider the total piece.

It is important to maintain the surface

that you worked so hard in the wax to get.

Keep your finishing to a minimum.

Remove sprues gates and vents with a

hacksaw, bolt cutter or a

large cold chisel.

It is hard work but you maintain the control.

There is no easy way that works safely.

Cut the sprues.

Do not break them off.

Breaking from the body is uncontrolled.

The break can tear into the body,

putting a cavity where you

don't want one.

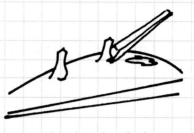

Chisel Stubs Flush

Remove the sprue stubs with

cold chisels, and/or

grinding stones or disks.

You can use an electric hand drill,

hand held grinder,

air driven flexible shaft or

a jewelry flexible shaft.

Go easy with the grinding.

For some reason grinders don't like to stop.

They like to put their mark everywhere.

Keep the grinding to an absolute minimum.

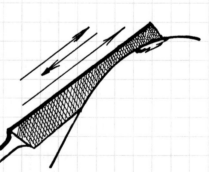

Remove the flashing and the bubbles with the cold chisel.

Less danger of error.

More control.

Easier to blend into the piece.

Blend with a file.

Blend With a File

Hammer texture into the piece.

A hammer can compress the metal

to blend in the grinding marks and

to blend in the chisel marks.

Use a ball peen hammer,

steel punches or

steel matting tools.

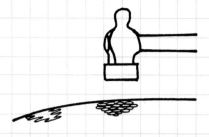

Hammer Texture Into the Piece

Make your own punches or matting tools to match the texture you need.

You can polish your piece if it is to big or heavy for the jewelry buffs.

Use car polishing disks and pads with

an electric hand drill.

Felt covered sticks or

chamois covered sticks are fast working.

Make your own stick 1″ to 4″ wide, and about 18″ long.

Rub the felt or chamois with bobbing compound.

Clean the metal with detergent and ammonia.

You can get a high polish with the rouge compound.

Be sure to use a different stick or

use chamois or felt like you were polishing shoes.

Rub with the compounds and strop away.

Use a different cloth for each compound.

Paint with oxides and

strop again with a clean cloth.

Paste wax will slow further oxidation.

SOME COMMON EXPERIENCES
AND PROBABLE REASONS WHY

Feathered edge.
   Too much debubblizer.
      Failed to blow excess off.
   Wax is hydro-static, it will attract water.
      If the wax is in the investment for a long period of time before the investment sets, this condition will occur.

Presence of large bubbles.
   Did not vibrate or vacuum enough.
   Did not use debubblizer.
   Did not allow air an escape route.
   Positioned the object so that it trapped air.

Stone fractured.
   Stone fractured before casting.
   Too much metal touching stone.
   Cooled stone too rapidly.
   Stone might not be castable.

Metal did not fill model.
   Weighted incorrectly.
   Poor burn out trapped air in mold.
   Incorrect sprueing.

Pits appear in metal.
   Thick/thin shrinkage.
   Points of plaster broke from model and floated to edge of metal.
      Caused by the presence of ashes.

Unintentional hollowed member.
   Massive metal areas will draw metal from thin adjoining areas.

Investment loose in flask.
   Mixture was too thin.

Metal broke through mold.
   Model too close to the top or side of mold.
   Flask was not filled to the top with investment.
   Flask was filled with different batches of investment.

YOUR JEWELRY SHOP
AND YOUR HEALTH

Is your shop vented the way it should be?
   YOUR JEWELRY SHOP IS A HAZARD AND DANGEROUS TO YOUR HEALTH.
   That is a fact.
   There is no avoiding that fact.
      Wear a practical mask for
         investment mixing,
            for buffing, and polishing and grinding.

Do you vent all those activities? Why not?
   Don't use acid without venting, and even then
      wear an organic filter mask,
      wear an eye guard, and
      wear an acid resistant apron.
   Wear an eye guard when casting.
   Wear a protective apron.
   Wear protective gloves.
   Use glasses or head gear with lenses for melting metal.

You don't need to do any of that, because you are careful?
   Who are you trying to kid.

Some of the dangers are obvious, like the acid being vented.
   Or like having plating solutions near acid baths.
   After all a burned lung or a whiff of cyanide gas; dead is dead, right?

Much of our danger is in the future. If you like making jewelry and would like to do it for a
   long time, perhaps you dream of retiring, and setting up a small shop in that city of your
   dreams. If you do, it is time that you paid attention to your polluted shop.

It is hard to take when you are told that all the processes of jewelry have become TOXIC to
   your body. That if you continue to work in that environment, you will, in a very short time
   become a basket case unable to take care of yourself.

Most of the danger can be solved by venting.
   Vents are easy to construct. Arrange for them to draw fumes away from you.
   As workers of metal, as problem solvers par excellence, we don't have any excuse except
      our own stupidity to believe that it can't happen to us.
   And it will happen to you if you don't take care and vent.

References for Additional Reading

Contemporary Jewelry by Morton (Holt, Rinehart Winston).

Creative Gold and Silversmithing by Choate (Crown Publishers).

Design and Creation of Jewelry by Von Neumann (Chilton).

Jewelry Making by Bovin (Bovin).

Metal Techniques for Craftsman by Untracht (Doubleday).

Jewelry Concepts and Technology by Oppi Untracht (Doubleday).

Penaland School of Crafts Book of Jewelry Making (Bobbs-Merrill).

Textile Techniques in Metal by Fish (Van Nostrand).

Creative Jewelry Techniques by O'Conner (Dunconnor).

The Jeweler's Bench Reference by O'Conner (Donconnor).

Form Emphasis for Metalsmiths by Seppa (Kent State University Press).

Centrifugal or Lost Wax Jewelry by Bovin (Bovin).

Jewelry, Contemporary Design and Technique by Evans (Davis).

The Complete Metalsmith by Tim McCreight

Metalworking for Jewelry by Tim McCreight

Modeling in Wax for Jewelry and Sculpture by Lawrence Kallenberg.

RECORD OF CASTING

Casting Flask Number	Weight of Wax	Weight of Metal	Kind of Metal	Kind Gem Cast	De-bubbl-ize?	Length of Burnout	Length of "Red Soak"	Condi-tion of Casting

INDEX

Alcohol lamp, 42, 43
Antiquing. See Oxidizing
Autoclave, 121

Bezel mount, 85-88
Birthstones, 96
Blaster, 36
Bowls, 33
Brass, 15
Broken arm machine, 133-135
Bronze, 15
Buffing, 156-60, 177
Buffing compounds, 157-59, 177
Buffs, 158-59
Buildup wax. See Wax, trailing
Bunsen burner, 42, 66
Burnisher, 28
Burn out, 70, 117-18, 119-32, 165, 173-74
Burrs, 29, 73
Buttons, 105-106

Candles, 41
Carving tools, 73
Carving wax, 72-73
Casting,
    centrifugal, 133-47
    gravity, 165-77
Casting, centrifugal vs. gravity, 165, 168, 170
Casting, cleaning of, 150-51, 175
Casting machines, 35, 133-40
Casting record, 125
Casting weight, 103-104, 165, 168
Clamps, 28
Cooling process, 118, 149, 175
Copper, 14
Craftsmanship, 8
Crown mounts, 80-81
Crucible furnaces, 143-45, 174
Crucibles, 35-36, 135, 138-39, 140, 174-75

Debubblization, 106-108, 114-17, 170, 171-72
Design, 3-6
Design modes, 7
Double boiler, 66
Drill bits, 28

Exploding investment, 125

Files, 27, 59, 73
Flask bases, 169-70
Flasks, 33
Flask temperature, prime, 131
Flat oval mount, 82
Flexible shafts, 30
Flux bomb, 145
Fluxes, 135, 138-39, 140-41
Form, 1-2
Furnaces, 36

Gas burner, 42-43
Gate sprue system, 165-68
Gauges, 31
Gemstones,
    castability of, 93-95
    cast-in-place, 81, 90-92
    glass, 96
    parts of, 79
    shapes of, 79
    synthetic, 94, 96
Gemstone setting, types of,
    bezel, 76
    prongs, 76-78
Gold, 12-14

Hammers, 28, 177
Heating devices, 41-46
Heat stages, 123-24, 173-74
Hot plate, 66, 122-23

Investing process, 105-118, 170-73
    preparing for, 105-109, 165-67
    vacuuming in, 114-17
    vibrating in, 117, 170
    water-to-investment ratio for, 109-114
Investment removal, 149-51, 175-76

Kilns, 120-22, 126-31
    electric, 122, 127-28, 130-31, 173-74
    gas, 122, 127-28, 130-31, 173
    wood, 122
Knives, 37-38, 65, 67, 69

Mandrels, 29, 66-67
Metal, properties of, 98-99
Metal weight, 9, 103-104

Nippers, 151

Organic materials, 70-71, 119
Oxidizing, 161-64, 177

Pits. See Porosity
Plastics, 69, 119
Platinum, 14
Pliers, 27
Polishing, 156-59, 177
Porosity, 99-100, 160, 169
Pressure cooker, 122
Probes, 37, 58, 60-61, 65
Prongs, 88-89
Pumice, 153
Pryometer, 120, 129
Pyrometric cones, 129-30

"Red soak" time, 120
Rings, finishing of, 154-56
Ruler, 131

Safety precautions, 66, 121, 122, 145, 147, 162, 163, 173
Sandpaper, 57, 59, 73, 74
Saws, 27, 69, 73
Scales, 31, 33
Silver, 10-12
Sprue cutters, 29
Sprue removal, 151, 175-76
Sprueing systems, 97-104, 165-68
Steel wool, 153-54
Stone pusher, 31
Straight arm machine, 139, 140, 143

Thermal shock, 90, 91, 92
Tongs, 149
Torches,
    acetylene, 47-49, 136
    gas-air, 47
    hydrogen-oxygen, 47
    oxygen-acetylene, 45
    oxygen-L.P. gas, 48
    oxygen-natural gas, 48, 50-51, 137

Trailing tools, 38-41
Tree sprue system, 168
Trumming, 159-60
Tweezers, 29

Vacuum casters, 34
Vacuum pump, 33, 114-17
Vent sprue system, 165-68
Vibrating table, 32, 115-17

Wax,
    dipping of, 65-67
    dripping of, 68
    finishing of, 74
    laying on, 65
    pouring of, 68
    trailing of, 62-64
Wax, types of,
    blue preformed shapes, 19-20
    file and carving, 24
    green casting sheets, 20
    green preformed shapes, 21
    green sticky sheets, 21
    master pattern, 22-23
    pink base plate, 18
    pink casting sheets, 18
    pink set up, 18
    pink sheet wax, 19
    trailing, 24-25
Wax gun, 44
Waxing tools, 37-38
Wax pens, 45-46
Wax sheets, 17
    carving on, 58, 72-73
    fabrication of, 55-56
    finishing edges of, 57
    forming over of, 54
    in gemstone setting, 85-89
    joining wire with, 58-59
    patterns in, 53-54
Wax wire,
    in gemstone setting, 80-83, 89
    joining of, 58-59, 103
    shaping of, 60-61